LEADING
IN RETAIL

The Humor and Art of Retail Leadership

BRIAN TRAVILLA

PAGE PUBLISHING, INC.
New York, NY

First originally published by Page Publishing, Inc. 2018

ISBN 978-1-64350-768-2 (Paperback)
ISBN 978-1-64350-769-9 (Digital)

Printed in the United States of America

My story is not special—it's just mine.

I dedicate this story to all the leaders and associates in retail. No matter your title, the type of shoes you may wear, or how many years you have worn a name tag, this book is for you.

We work way too much and do amazing things every day, all while wearing a name tag.

I also want to dedicate this heartwarming book to my wife, Charlene, and three boys, Nicolas, Aiden, and Parker, because they have given up so many hours of time for my schedule and my devotion to writing this book.

Let him that would move the world first move himself.

—Socrates

CONTENTS

FOREWORD

Please allow me to introduce myself. My name is Brian Travilla, and I have never written a book. So this immediately makes me an expert. I have wanted to write this book for quite a few years as I gained more experience, the more experiences and life lessons in retail I wanted to share. I am not going to give you a five-step process to becoming a vice president. I will indeed share with you my failures, a sprinkling of my successes, and more—my vision of how leaders make mountains move.

Have you ever worked directly for a person that had the term "manager" on their name tag? I know you have, and take a moment to reflect if that person managed you or led you. There is a remarkably large difference between managing and leading that, at times, we tend to put aside. Grunting the days and weeks out to make a sales plan or a financial budget gives us the blinders to forget when the last time was when someone noticed you. You are working very hard these days, and as our world evolves, there is a significant need for leaders to rise and inspire. We have been managed for far too long, and besides the cool start-up companies that fashion beards, craft beer Fridays, and ping-pong tables. Perhaps you may be working for a large or small corporation that reports earnings each quarter, and it may seem that companies want more and more, yet the resources are becoming scarcer. This is indeed the calling for leaders!

Let's get back to why I am writing this book. I have over twenty-six in retail and currently twenty-six years as a leader from my humble beginnings as a significantly underpaid department manager rising through the ranks of a senior leader. All in all, I have always noticed the little things and paid attention to the vast amounts of extraordinarily around me. I have totally screwed up before and drank from the chalice or, rather, the Dixie cup of victory too. So my goal in this book is to get you thinking about where you are as a manager and help you grow you. (Trust me, there isn't anyone out there waiting to promote you.) You will have to find this energy within yourself, for it is there right now.

Hang on tight, I will probably skip all over the place, and as you finish the read, you may chuckle a few times, look inside yourself, and with all hope, start leading!

CHAPTER ONE

Why Retail?
Defining a Pathway for Challenge
and Success

High expectations are the key to everything.
—Sam Walton, founder of Walmart

Retail is kind of a funny business. I can't think of a business more up and down than retail sales. Thinking about how nearly everything hinges on the retail sector market, from stocks to GDP, retail has its hands in nearly everything. Yet within the retail world, there is quite a diverse segment of employees.

Let's start with my humble and rather blissful beginnings: the hourly associate. None more valuable, the hourly associate clearly is the mortar that binds the bricks of any retailer. I was hired as a part-time housewares associate in 1992 for the ripe hourly wage of $4.50. This job was grueling. I was simply associate no. 98611 working in a large department store. I had earned a 9 before my true associate number due to the fact I could earn a small commission if, and that is if I sold a warranty on small home appliances and ceiling fans. I would ask every customer, "For $4.99, this $19.99 toaster is covered for two years! Would you like to add this to your toaster?" The customer typically replied, "No!" Needless to say, I was a grunt that felt quite defeated each time I offered this gosh-darn warranty. I would often gaze at the full-time commission associates (typically people in their mid- to late forties) and wonder just how they got that far up in the store. I would retreat back to my dungeon of a department as I only had six pallets of freight to process within my 5:00 to 9:00 p.m. shift.

Those commission-based associates would earn more from one sale than I would earn in a week, breaking my back, wearing a tie I had no clue how to tie. (Back in those days, my dear millennials, neither Google nor the internet was around to learn this kind of stuff.) So a square knot it was. Yet I was, and continue to be, a dreamer and said to myself, "One day, I will be their boss." How ignorantly cocky of me to skip over the sales portion and go right to boss, eh? So I banged out pallet after pallet and quickly realized this was clearly not for me. Those darn splinters you get when you have to pick the pallet up are just brutal. Oh, be careful of the nails too.

Another one of my duties included mixing paint, and I absolutely hated this task. Imagine it is a Saturday, and some great DIY dude walks in and says, "I want six gallons of exterior paint, and I want um . . . eh . . . errs . . . this color." "Right away, sir," I kindly replied. When I approached this 1947 manual death trap of a paint mixer, it never worked. I would mix the paint precisely as how I was taught in thirty-second training seminar, and the color *never* matched. After about nine or so gallons, I got it right. "Danger! Danger! Boss en route!" Just as I conquered the paint, my boss would literally chew me out for damaging so much paint tint. I received a good old-fashioned threat, yell, nearly a scream, and "Fix it next time or you're fired" chew-out. Let's just forgo the root-cause analysis and go right to personally threatening a sixteen-year-old that was working like a rented mule. I then officially fell in love with retail.

As time passed, I learned the value of communication with customers. In fact, those darn warranties were a personal challenge to me. No one sold too many, and I was determined to sell these versus work pallets. (Could this be the start of critical thinking? Let's not get too confident just yet.) I quickly learned why customers buy things and found the right way to simply offer the right solution: they officially needed a two-year replacement warranty! I was able to start conversations with customers three times my age on the proper usage of a fan or toaster and connect the dots of ease and convenience with our warranty. In fact, I made it a goal to sell a minimum of five warranties per shift. Funny thing is, when my sixteen-year-old mind established a goal, I started to meet this additional sale challenge. I watched my fellow compadres work freight like crazy, and I volunteered to help those "pesky" customers. Whenever I saw customers, I would jump to help them. My peers would laugh and oddly keep working while I marathoned customers as long as I could. I sold so many warranties that my boss approached me and asked what I was doing differently. I simply replied, "I'm ensuring they get what they need versus what they want." He didn't believe me as he snarled and walked away. Remember, I earned roughly a quarter to fifty cents for each warranty I sold, so now I was making some serious money. I was averaging $6.00 per hour versus my laborious peers at $4.50. Hmmm, goals. I was starting to learn that hard work is great, but selling and talking to customers is far better!

My store manager even made the rare appearance from his office to ask me (impersonally looking at my name tag prior to talking), "How are you selling these warranties?" I offered the same reply, and he simply said, "Nice job. One day when you are older, you can sell in the commission departments." I said, "Thanks, sir, but I would rather manage the department." He didn't talk to me again.

This was a humbling lesson for me at a very young age. While I had the vision to lead early in my career, I didn't see (yet) the value in earning my way to the top. This might sound a bit old-fashioned, but working your way from the basement on up is an admiral approach. Mind you, it is the long way around the lake, yet it offers a great deal of experience.

I eventually started to sell as a 100 percent commission sales associate. No more pallets! Talk about competitive. I was eighteen and selling furniture with the big dogs, the alpha males and females. How could this be difficult? Perhaps I overlooked a small data point. I didn't even own any furniture at eighteen years old. I was still living under the wing of my mother. Nonetheless, it was my time to shine. I learned quickly to make conversation with people and practice one key attribute of salesmanship: you must always use your name when you introduce yourself to anyone that is a potential customer. Why? People will feel more comfortable with people they know. Your name is the first and foremost path to comfort within a sale.

Let me give you the playing field so you can understand the nature of this business. On any given Saturday or Sunday, there were at least ten to fifteen sales associates all vying for the same dollar. Many of these sales associates have families, bills, dreams, and responsibilities. Here I am, eighteen, with nothing to lose. Needless to say, I wasn't the fan favorite. Working on commission teaches you a few things.

1. Get comfortable shoes.
2. Your feelings are left in the break room.
3. The first no from a customer always means there is a need for more information in order to make a buying decision.
4. The best customers always visit you on your lunch, and some other lucky person gets your sale.
5. People come and go.

I had to quickly learned how to sell and make money. Yet I wasn't satisfied. I felt the desire to lead and coach my fellow salespeople. Even though I was young and rather ignorant, I knew I wanted to lead others versus sell products. There was one problem though. Our department had just received a new manager, and she was determined to make a big splash, and I was sure to get a promotion. Damn. I continued to sell, make a great paycheck, and watch every move this new manager was making. In time, it was clear that this manager was not enjoying herself. She was more accustomed leading noncommissioned associates. She did not have the tough conversations to getting into the guts of the business. The sales force was eating her for lunch. Leading commission associates is similar to being a prison guard in the jail yard. Only the strongest survive.

After about a year, I was still selling and skipping lunches to catch the pesky customer that always seemed to visit during this time. But now I was a fully functional, mildly successful, and cocky-as-the-day-is-long nineteen-year-old young man. I had seen it all, or so I had thought. From near fistfights to associates smoking too many cigarettes to more BS stories than I could handle, I was indeed ready to earn that shiny gold name tag, Manager. One day I came to work and was ready to start my shift. My now fourth store manager called me to his office and asked if I was happy with the company. I replied with a subdued, "Yes." He asked me if I felt I was ready to be a manager. I exclaimed, "Yes!" He made a phone call and confirmed with I suspect was a regional or district manager and then looked at me and stated that I was now the manager of the second largest department within the store. All for a significant salary of twenty-five thousand dollars. I instantly responded with, "I accept, and thank you." I was in what I will call thirteenth grade at a local community college, and as I accepted this new position, I was delighted to immediately drop out of college and start my rocket-launched career as a manager at approximately nineteen and a half years old.

As you can imagine, all my coworkers now instantly hated me. I was the person in charge and could tell them what to do and when to do it. I will admit I was cautious to let any type of power go to my head, for by nature, I am a pretty mild dude. Everyone still hated me because I was now a manager and no longer a friend or coworker. This was a trying time for me personally and quite isolating. Opening, closing, working all the time by myself, and watching my friends always going out after work was hard. I had to decline any offer to join because I was their leader and wasn't permitted to mix with the employees. This granted me time to reflect on my past and build a plan for my future. Keep in mind, I had left school to be a full-time manager and felt my life was coming together professionally in a very rich way. Yet my personal life was imbalanced and, well, very lonely.

As I was ascending through the junior ranks of management, I started to tackle more complex issues that continued to develop my technical skills. An absolutely fantastic regional vice president (whom, to this very day, I admire and owe such a great deal of gratitude to) observed me during a store visit and saw a glimmer of hope. I was being sent to other stores to help with merchandising and sales education. Then I was assigned to work with newly promoted managers on the basic training of how to be a manager. Wow. How in the heck did I land this? Here I was at twenty years old teaching! My regional vice president at that time must have seen some kind of potential in me as I was making the journey to becoming a leader.

I flew to Chicago to visit my father late summer of 1997. I was eager to visit a store within my company located near his home office, wanting to see a big store in a big city. I was amazed that this store was two stories and had more associates than I had ever seen. To my delight, I saw a former peer manager in Florida that had transferred to Chicago. We caught up, and I shared just how amazed I was with the glamour of the big city and the intensity of the business. Growing up in Florida, we just didn't move this fast. My friend said that he had heard that human resources was looking for candidates to transfer to Chicago. In a reflective and quite naive manner, I burst out, "I would transfer here in a heartbeat."

On the Wednesday prior to Black Friday of 1997, I received a phone call from a human resources manager asking me if I had expressed an interest in moving to Chicago. "Yes," I said. She then offered me a position as a large department manager at a store that was going through a large remodel to chart a new course for the company within Chicago. I paused for roughly three microseconds before replying, "I accept."

Within an instant, my life changed in nearly every possible way.

We will get back to me a bit later. For now, let's move on to learning more about the differences between leaders and managers.

Thinking: the talking of the soul with itself.
—Plato

CHAPTER TWO

Managing versus Leading
The Fundamental Difference in Both

To be technical (at least by my definition—remember, this isn't a technical book), a *manager* is one who manages process or people to accomplish a task, while a *leader* is one who inspires role models and encourages the very best from people who accomplish tasks.

If the end result is the same, what is the difference? Seems that if one gets others to work, it is a win-win? Not even close.

Let's talk about managers for a bit. Think of a process-oriented businesses. From fast food to grocery stores, you need to hustle to get things done. Time is money, and money is elusive, so move even quicker. I can see the need for a talented individual to impart their knowledge to subordinate workers to ensure everyone does their tasks correctly. Makes sense. When you work somewhere for a while, you learn how to do things, you do these things for a long time, and then some poor soul grants you the title of manager. I can imagine you are shaking your head right now and saying out loud, "Damn, this is totally true!" The issue here is that the talented or enduring person who was just promoted may not have shown any people skills but, rather, only technical skills. To keep things easy, we will imagine a fast-food restaurant. The longer I cook food, the better I have become. Cooking burgers and fries may not be difficult, but let's face it, it is tough work, day in and day out. The people that have the staying power typically get promoted. I am not stating in any way that long-term associates who are promoted to manager are in any way a bad choice, for in many cases, it is 100 percent the right choice. (However, the talent that is promoted is technical skill and simply tenure.) Skills are teachable, and tenure is typically viewed as a rite of passage and even a pedestal.

The new manager usually wants to change everything so that everyone does things his way versus the best way. Again, emotion, ego, and opportunity play a key role here. Anyone who decries anything against the new manager is generally outcast, performance managed, or fired. Are you seeing a path here? Managers tend to manage processes and not necessarily people. Those bothersome associates get in the way of the process! Day in and day out, the manager keeps a watchful eye on process improvement, expense control, and timely customer service. All very good areas to monitor. Yet where is the focus on the employee or the values of the team?

Some managers are potentially the best process innovators. They thrive on taking complex processes and making them easier to do. (Or at least the employees want to believe this.) Let's face it, imagine the process of building a skyscraper. There are hundreds of processes that all must work together to ensure safety, accuracy, financial estimates, and ultimately the finished product. This requires someone to ensure everything is in harmony and on the budgeted time schedule. Without management, we could imagine the chaos.

I have quite a bit of experience with construction project managers. They are often in a bad mood, have a likening for plaid shirts, and fashion a customized hard hat. Yet in working with these managers, they have a knack, almost a sixth sense of getting things done. They are meticulous, cantankerous, effective, and extremely dedicated to the job. No matter the day of week or time of day, I have seen these managers committing everything they have to getting the project done. They finish the job, take little to no credit, and drive to their next project. Many managers within different fields possess these qualities. Consider a military field sergeant, quite possibly the most valued player on the team. They just wear a different type of hard hat. Selfless, dedicated, and determined experts.

Management is typically the foundational element of leadership. People often choose the path to grow from being an individual contributor, meaning they accomplish work independently or in small groups, or they evolve to leading others to do so. Both are admirable, yet there is a difference. Referencing my first chapter, when you become skilled at a task, you either continue to do this task and make a living or you may be given the opportunity of leading the task. Far too many times, it is the fear of letting go of comfort in task that leads people to stay as an individual contributor. Remember, this is okay. The flip side is a neurotic manager that cannot let go and micromanages everything you do. This makes me want to rip phone books in half. I have been fortunate to have only seen and dealt with a few of these in my time. (Whew.) Yet I have worked with many as a peer and simply observed these managers as they burn out to a point of no return. They often live in a perpetual state of being pissed off at basically everything.

Learning to manage takes time. You need to invest this time or you will be received as an ignorant manager who leads through title and not acumen. Be careful! You might fit this profile right now as you read this. Think about what you have done to get here and what you may need to do to flip the coin over and start a new path. You can do it. It just takes self-reflection, determination, and a good dose of humility.

Story time.

In a previous position in Florida, I was a twenty-two-year-old manager for a large company recently transferred to Chicago, Illinois, as the hardlines manager of a focal store. I thought I was the best of the best. Now let's break this down a bit. Being twenty-two gives you extremely limited life experience and historical references to recall. Yet being promoted to the big city told me that I was the best. As I reflect, I was the perhaps the most courageous of my peers. Moving from Florida to Chicago in December is just a stupid move. Trust me.

In my new position, I was working with a diverse team of tenured and new associates. Yet in the back of my mind, I was thinking that I was the best. I didn't know it then, but I was showing it. I was acting like a total ——hole. I was telling people what to do, giving orders, all while being hands-off. I was clearly a major jerk. (To give more detail about my team.) I was used to managing around twenty-five associates in Florida (sun, sand, and complete awesomeness), and now in Chicago (cold, traffic, grit, and crazy busy) I was managing fifty to seventy-five associates. Not only was I in over my head, I was greatly outnumbered.

In a matter of days, I went from managing in a small southern store where everyone knew me to managing in an urban city store where no one knew me. Based on my behavior, I figured they were plotting my death. I took very little time to get to know my staff, their names, family, goals, talents, dreams, or even their passions (as to why they work for the same company).

I was surrounded by bigger bosses, and because I wanted to be one, I started to act like one. At least I thought I was acting like a bigger boss. Bear in mind, I was getting the job done and done well. Yes, making my sales plans and managing labor properly. The associates did what I asked and did it well. My direct boss was happy with my results and didn't spend much time with me, so I presumed he was happy. Okay, if A equals doing a good job and boss is happy, and B equals department is running smoothly and everyone is working hard, then C must equal to *I* am feeling great and I am leading a huge team and doing well. So A + B = C! (I never passed prealgebra in school, so I am impressed with my algebraic example here.)

Let's look a bit deeper and ask a few questions:

1. Did I mention anything about spending time with my associates to get to know what motivates and drives their passions? No.
2. Did I mention anything about teaching and training my team to do things better or to gain their insights as to how we should proceed? No.
3. Did I mention that my direct leader was spending time with me on teaching me how to be a better manager? No.

This is a dangerous and shortsighted situation. I was taking all the energy and effort from my team and not giving anything back. Eventually, my team was not being led, but they were giving me their best and I wasn't, and it was 100 percent my fault.

As a youthful manager, I was enthralled with a nice suit, an office, and a nice car. I had just one nice suit that I wore way too much and an overpriced car that was horrible to drive in Chicago winters. After the newness of the big city wore off, I was realizing that I wasn't the best of the best, nor was I happy. I had not learned that the value I would place within my team would immediately be paid by way of positive growth, having a humble mind, appreciating the joy of seeing others growing, and learning and trying new things. My personal pronoun was still *me*, not *us*.

Roughly a year into my Chicago journey, the company I was working for was definitely hitting rough times. Things were changing very quickly, and morale was desperately low in the stores and in the field. I started to get a sense that it was time to look for a new job. Being in my early twenties, I had guts. However, I was missing a crucial piece: experience and intelligence. Despite the missing pieces, I quickly found a new job and one that promised to keep me moving forward in the ranks.

I took a few days to get my courage mustered, and then I submitted my resignation one morning to the vice president of the region. I was immediately dismissed from my job and strangely walked out to my car that morning and felt just weird. Wow, I did not see that coming. (I quickly learned that oftentimes when managers resign, they are dismissed that very moment.) Remember, I am still a manager here, and nowhere have I even touched the art of leading.

At now, twenty-three years old, I took a few days between jobs to reflect on my past eight years and try to place it all in the right framework of where I wanted to go. While tremendously eager, I was still and continue to be very reflective. Leadership rule no. 32: take time to contemplate on where you have been and where you are going.

I reflected on all the great associates and managers I had worked with at the first company I worked for and the long-lasting relationships I had established. I did help others grow, and I even taught quite a few people how to do things better. Yet I didn't have enough experience to understand the hows and whys of adding value to a team. Perhaps my shortsightedness wasn't intentional but more me clawing my way through the business world. Hmmmm, sound familiar?

Some points to touch on prior to ending this chapter are the following:

- New managers and leaders can value different things as more experienced managers and leaders.
- It is okay to make mistakes—that is, if you learn from them and stay humble.
- Nothing is perfect and everything has a cost.

My early twenties were tough. Many of my friends were enjoying college and then graduation with a number of options for their jobs and lives. I chose the earn-as-you-go method. Not one way is right or wrong, just different. And again, that is okay.

Connecting the Dots

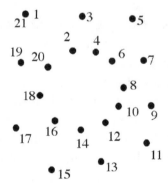

The goals for this chapter are intended to inspire you to think about yourself and how you are currently managing or leading. You may need a complete overhaul or just a few finishing touches. A leader is one who will recognize talent and help it grow. A manager will ensure the capability is present to accomplish the task.

Which one sounds better to you?

> Your name tag is like a pair of pants, can't
> come to work without them.

CHAPTER THREE

Do I Really Have to Wear a Name Tag?
Yes, You Do

Early in my career, I was issued a name tag. I felt so lucky that someone else made my name tag. I mean, someone took the time to make it display BRIAN. It was made with the old-fashioned circled thing you hold in your hand and the top had a dial that you find each letter and press it. (Those of you born before 1980 might understand what I am explaining.) It was the groovy maroon color and had a pin that would make a nice hole in your shirt every damn time you put it on. Despite the treacherous result of holy shirts, I wore this maroon name tag with pride. Through the years, the size and color would change as I gained more experience. At one point, my name tag was gold with the large embossed title of MANAGER on it. Now I was in heaven.

I would imagine that many years ago, one smart person decided that a name tag would allow the employees and customers to call each other by name. This was the secret sauce that would improve customer service, right? No. If I had a crisp one-dollar bill for every time I had to remind an associate or manager to wear their name tag or I had to hear a fateful story of how it was lost in the washing machine, fell off, broke, was stolen, or was a product of an elaborate scheme that involved alien life-forms, I would be retired by now.

In reality, the name tag should be the starting point for a customer or associate to learn your name. I find this practice of using your name when you meet people going the way of the dinosaur. Too many times, we text, e-mail, or simply say hello in a very impersonal nature. Looking at someone in their eyes and saying "Hi, my name is Brian" seems to be difficult and socially awkward for our younger team members. The name tag is here to stay, and we simply need to accept it.

Nowadays, name tags come with nifty magnetic backers that have mercy on shirts. Yet it still is a name tag. Think of professions that require employees to wear the venerable name tag. For example:

- Doctors.
- Police officers.
- Retail employees.
- Service industry (food).
- Realtors.
- Teachers with lanyards and pins! (This one is for you, Mom. ☺)
- Janitorial and automotive professionals even get their names embroidered on their shirt!
- Corporate folks have those credit card name tags, fashioned with pictures and stickers hanging from their belts and pants that make you look at their name within areas of their person that is a bit uncomfortable.
- Military personnel.

All are valued professions that still use the good ole name tag and make a difference every day. So is it the name tag that is the difference maker? Probably not, but we will continue to explore here.

Name tag rule no. 42: Don't put it on upside down. No one will tell you, and you will discover it later in the day and feel foolish.

Name tag rule no. 37: Ensure it is aligned and proper. A crooked name tag looks messy and sends a micro message that you may not care about details. If it becomes scratched, chewed on, burned, bent, or broken, ask or even pay for a new one. (Cheapskate.)

Name tag rule no. 21: If possible, wear your name tag on your left breast so when you meet someone and shake their hand, they shake your right hand and look left for your name. It just fits.

I find that having a few is essential. Too many times I have visited a store and had to ask the question of questions. "Can you please make me a name tag?" The store manager gives me a look of astonishment and gets it done. Nowadays, I wear just a basic one with no title. Just Brian. I have learned a thing or two and find that a title can present a barrier to subordinates and customers. I feel strongly that if people know me as Brian, then I get the best from them. If people know me as a title, then, well, they may just do what I ask. Big difference indeed.

Learning Time

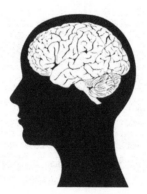

You may never get used to wearing a name tag. It's okay. They are probably going away soon anyway. So I ask that next time you see an upside-down name tag, say and do nothing. It always makes me giggle a few minutes later. For that poor soul was probably on their way to work setting record speeds and just trying to get things done. Upside down, that is.

> The hands and toes you step on climbing up the corporate ladder are connected to the ass you kiss falling down. (Gregg Travilla [Although he most likely didn't invent this, he taught this saying to me.])

Prior to this chapter, I want to share another thought with you.

In our professional lives, we all tend to ebb and flow. That is, every day is different, and let's be honest, who comes to work with the exact same mental and physical effort each day? As long as you have significantly more positive days than negative days, life is pretty good.

CHAPTER FOUR

Please and Thank You

Have you ever been told what to do? At times, this is extraordinarily necessary. Let's think about some instances that might be suitable:

- Boot camp in any type of military unit
- Shooting a weapon for the very first time, i.e., "Point that way" (please)
- Driving a car with a nervous parent for the first time in traffic
- Learning CPR
- Landing an airplane
- Learning to tie your shoes
- Those college days learning the art of a keg stand

I think you get the point. At times, being told is a highly effective teaching method. Balanced with feedback and a sprinkling of recognition, it typically never hurts. In fact, many people do very much enjoy following others orders. This brings a sense of control and stability to many people that may not be able to create that for themselves.

However, there are many examples that telling people what to do is seen and felt as harsh, course, and just downright mean. It is generally social norm to utilize the verbiage "Please and thank you."

Yet it is far more of a norm that most humans rarely say "Please" and even better luck getting a "Thank you." Why?

I am not a psychologist nor did I ever take sociology. However, I have spent the better part of my life shoulder to shoulder with leaders of all sorts. Ones that make millions of dollars each year to ones who are happy the last ramen noodle in the cupboard wasn't shrimp flavor. Nonetheless, I cannot draw a line that would say anything financial or even level of education discerns one that is polite by nature.

I will add that upbringing and a personal sense of feeling good about oneself is a good start. So is it necessary to be so darn polite with people you see every day? If you say anything other than yes, you are kindly asked to read this chapter twice.

Let's consider how people feel when they are treated with a respectful approach. A positive tone is set, a mind is opened, and the can-do approach is typically reciprocated. Looking back to our chapter "Leaders versus Managers," would it be safe to say that, at times, managers may tend to tell versus ask? Consider the functional level of acumen of many managers. This brings the operation to the forefront versus the people actually doing the work. It is easy to treat people as a function of the operation. For example, if productivity is slowing on a factory assembly line, a manager may verbally nudge or actually yell to the team to speed things up. If the energetic words are meant to help, that may be the right course of action. Yet energies crest and fall. If you choose the yelling method, expect your productivity and engagement to do the same. One note: If your team is slacking off, a good scrape may be needed. However, always think about the whys. Why does my team feel it is okay to slack off? Or why does my team not find value in their work? Bigger picture, why isn't the team finding value in my direction or expectation?

Hard work stems from belief in the work or being physically monitored that when one stops working hard, they are physically assaulted. I will go out on a limb and say that the greater majority of us want to believe in our work. We want to feel connected to the inputs and results. Yet at times we stray, or we feel overwhelmed or even darn right dejected. While I shan't stem total dissatisfaction from being polite, being nice is the foundation to feeling good, and feeling good breeds, well, more good.

So what does it take to start being a nice person? Quite a bit. Let's start with your personal beliefs on communication. Are you an aggressive, no-nonsense person that deals with facts and only wants to straight scoop? Or more of a talkative person that enjoys the art of wordsmith? There is no right way, but your way and being mindful of your tendencies can help you communicate better and get more out of discussions. Slowing down or speeding up your dialogue to fit the other person's style is helpful and serves as a polite method to exchange. Also, you get more out of the conversation for the recipient is more at ease and will clearly offer more.

Focus on your discussions with your peers and friends, and take mental note if your circle or peeps use polite communication. Be careful not to get to cozy with people for forgetting general pleasantries erodes the foundation of the relationship. Start incorporating the P&T (please and thank you) slowly but regularly. If you, all of a sudden, start to use these words, people will definitely know you read this book. ☺ So in your own way, slide in the P&Ts, and this will certainly start a trend with your circle. You will notice that many people will follow your kindness, and then here is where the magic happens . . . Wait for it . . . Almost there . . . You will see people interacting in a respectful manner, and the mood of the company, team, or platoon will simply be better. And better begets better. The more you and your team or family shows outward respect, the positivity grows from inside. You will almost guarantee yourself to feel and act better.

Big picture, incorporate an honest and sincere "Please" and "Thank you" as much as you can. The worst people can say is, "Man, that guy is so darn polite I trust him." In reality, they will respect and take you as a person of honor.

So here is a story to share.

One day I had to do a planogram whilst a venerable electronics manager with a large department company. As an eager, young, and arrogant manager, I was entrusted to reset the entire furniture and appliance department in a day. (Yes, the electronics manager also had the esteemed pleasure of leading the furniture dudes.) Furniture sales people are just fantastic people. They spend their entire day tired, with sore feet surrounded by comfortable beds, couches, chairs, and such, but can never sit on them. Total torture. These folks used to spend their lives selling furniture and making a damn good living doing so. However, I digress.

So here I am, needing to move every gosh-darn washer, dryer, stove, and refrigerator. Talk about an act of futility. Just because it is here and not there, we are going to sell more? Some crazy buyer must have gotten a nice deal on a certain vendor for, strangely, all of one brand was mysteriously at the front.

One point to bear in mind is that the teams that I had to assemble to help me move sixty or so pieces of heavy and cumbersome equipment were commissioned associates. These folks were like furniture sales people but grumpier. They had mastered the appliance lean. Every time I would see these folks selling of doing whatever, they would lean on the appliance. (It's a good way to rest your dogs.) Oh, they were also not paid a dime to move anything. They were remunerated for selling, not moving. So I had to persuade these trusted souls to help. Let's give it a try. "Okay, gang, we need to do the planograms. Let's start with washers. They are freaking difficult and never move easy." (Even when you open the lid and scoot them on the side.) I was warmly responded with a loud "No, we are not moving shit." I stated they were being unprofessional and I was giving an order. This garnered an even louder "No." Major dilemma. I stated that we needed to get it done and it was good for them to move stuff around so we can sell more. Believe me, these (absolutely fantastic) associates have seen many young managers in their day and, by the way, have done the planograms a hundred times and probably haven't seen a sales lift.

Anyway, I had to assess the situation here. I was clearly outnumbered, dealing with a team that was smarter and much more experienced than I and were not too happy with my approach. So I resorted to guerilla tactics. I asked the team nicely for help, and strangely, one of my associates that was over twice my age said, "Brian, we will do anything for you if you just learn to say please." This was shocking to me. I couldn't believe this feedback. First, the fact that in the business world, I had to be polite and sensitive, and second, I actually had people around me that wanted to help me. Two very important life lessons for me. In the end, we spent the greater part of the day moving the damn appliances to the desired locations and sold a ton of them. I have learned that when you move lots of stuff, people buy more. My associates made more money and probably had sore backs, but we had a ton of fun that day.

See the Big Picture

You will most certainly get more done by being nice versus being a jerk. Sure, sometimes situations call for do-it-now behavior. However, we are typically not in those types of situations sitting in an office or serving a customer. Take a moment and keep your ego and mouth in check and say "Please and thank you," dammit.

Inspiration . . . move me brightly . . . light the songs
of sense and color . . . hold away despair.
—The Grateful Dead

CHAPTER FIVE

The Value of Inspiration

The word *inspiration* just sounds and feels good, doesn't it? Yet we often take the act of inspiration rather lightly. In this chapter (perhaps one of my favorites), we will explore many different examples of inspiration and how it has a dramatic effect on outcomes, feelings, belief, and plain old effort. You may be able to correlate points from the previous chapter on leaders versus managers. (That is, if you are paying attention and not taking three months to read this book I have poured my soul into!)

> [in-spuh-**rey**-shuh n] - influence directly and imme-
> diately exerted upon the mind or soul.

Let's dig into this explanation a bit. Influence that gets things going potentially from a positive place—this is already sounding productive. Really like the touch with mind and soul. Thinking of influencing the mind and soul, could there be a limit to what you could do if you were influenced such as this?

Ask yourself, when was the last time that you can remember when you were inspired? Not inspired to exercise or diet, but I mean straight-to-the-guts inspired. Besides the annual corporate meeting and clapping your hands for the boss throughout the day. I mean eye-to-eye, shoulder-to-shoulder inspired. Be careful on what to define or internalize as inspiration. Listening to a song, watching a movie, annual corporate meeting, they all potentially get you motivated and pumped up. Yet motivation is like a firecracker. It is colorful, makes you say "Ooh" and "Awww," and makes a loud noise. Then it is over. Inspiration is internal and very personal. Let's think of some things that might be motivation dressed as inspiration:

- A nice salary or bonus.
  - Money will come to you if and only if you work hard and make others better. Eventually, you will get used to the salary and bonus and the only goal will be to get more. This may not be inspiration.
- Keynote speaker that was super fun to listen to and made all your problems seem petty and easily overcome.
  - Darn those pesky speakers. They are just awesome at making large-scale problems seem so small. Consider their words, and then realize you have to take action to fix things. The speaker may have been charming, yet this feels more like motivation to change.
- New boss that is nice to you and knows your name.
  - New bosses freak everyone out. Getting one that is immediately personable is a huge bonus. One that learns and uses your name is a gift. Yet such a small act of decency should not inspire you. You are better that this. Increase your standards!
- Better work-life balance.
  - This is a tough one. For it rides the lines with salary and bonus. At first, the relief of time constraints will feel great. The open calendar will make you feel like a freed prisoner. Yet you will grow accustomed to this lifestyle and again want more.

All the above are nice and enjoyable within their own energies. Yet are you feeling inspired? I hope not. Now, let's think of some examples of potential inspiration:

- A mentor that knows you for who you are and is a constant teacher.
- A friend that has the ability to be there for you in good times and bad.
- Enjoying nature and fundamental elements of what this earth offers. (When was the last time you watched [in person] a sun rise?)
- Giving your time and energy to a good cause.
- Dreaming of what your future can be.

Interesting on these examples, for they are all basically free. They do not involve things. Wait, I thought we were all doing our jobs to get better and more stuff, right? Honestly, yes. However, inspiration may come in many forms. But the very best may be free.

Let's shape some examples of how you very well might start to be more aware of your value of inspiration to others. Again, by reading this book, you are most likely a manager or leader that is working on growing your skills. So I will take this example to expand.

Have you ever worked for someone that you just clicked? It feels great, and at times, you might have felt that the world had no limits. Your leader either gave you such great autonomy or just a ton of tutelage that you felt like you grew stronger and stronger each day? Would you classify this as inspiration? Absolutely!

Consider how you approach your team and how you empower these brave souls to be their best. Wait, back up—"to be their very best"? Or might you be the manager that is trying the get the best job done by your people? Would it even be possible to get the same or even more work done by your team if you changed course a bit and started to lead them to be their very best? This sounds fluffy and darn risky. We have to remember that you are in charge of a team and your job depends on their quality and quantity of work. So let's stay on the safe course and just make sure we do the annual performance appraisal by saying "Try harder, do better." If you agree with this, please gently put this book down and give it to someone else. You need a leadership intervention! In reality, inspiration shouldn't be planned but found and fostered.

Okay, now that we have that taken care of, imagine if your focus grew from only productivity to developing the talents of your team. What could you accomplish? More accurately, what couldn't you accomplish? This is a snare trap that tooooooooooooo many managers get caught in. We oftentimes are not willing to be different than the last manager and are just fine with staying the course. However, the few leaders that are keenly aware that the better their team is, the more they are connected with their work, the result is better and more completed. You might be saying to yourself right now, "I, um, do this every day!" No, you don't. Or "I have regular meetings with my staff and I know them well. I know the names of their kids!" Good for you. Still nada!

There is a huge difference between being a nice person and being an inspirational person. We know what nice is, so I will tell a short story.

I was a leader for a company, and I had a boss that was a very nice person. It was cool. We spoke infrequently, and when we did, it was always just conversational. This boss would see me just a few times a year, and things were easy with him. Yet I didn't do much growing. Bear in mind, if I needed him, he was there. But I never felt truly aligned and well-connected with him. I worked hard for him and offered many ideas for business improvement or growing sales. He typically listened and gave a good head nod. That was about it. During my annual performance appraisal, I always wondered how we wrote it. He never really spent time with me and didn't see me in action too much. But as you may guess, the reviews went fine. When he was promoted, I was bummed, but not sad. I was eager to get a new boss that would want to spend more windshield time together, get to know me. Challenge me. Disagree with me. I may sound needy. However, when you are not inspired by someone, motivation fills in, and motivation is fleeting.

Here is a gut check for you. When was the last time you took a moment during the day to provide on-the-spot coaching or feedback to a subordinate? I am not talking about corrective behavior like, "Do it this way." I am looking for "James, I observed you talking with one of your associates, and what I really liked was that you personalized your coaching to her. I could see that the suggestions you gave, Sally really connected with, and she was eager to try. Nicely done! You are really starting to get your coaching skills honed. I am going to keep my eye on you." How would you feel if you received anything even close to this example? You can tell that the leader is paying attention to his team. He is in the details. Here is another example: "Jennifer, I am confident that you are ready for this assignment. In fact, you have been for some time now. It is perfectly normal to be nervous. In fact, I still get nervous too when I take on more responsibility. The one wish I have for you is to keep your lines of communication open to your associates. You tend to get a little quiet when you are new to something. Believe in yourself, because I most certainly do!"

While these examples may sound nice or soft, inspiration doesn't have to be on a battlefield. Paying attention to your team and giving them clarity and belief goes a long way. By doing this, you are placing the responsibility on them to do a great job versus you overseeing them getting the job done. There is a big difference, right?

Inspiration often comes to us in subtleties. You may need to change your focus a bit on this one. If you are in charge of a sales team, in addition to measuring sales and head count, consider measuring where everyone on team's potential is and how you can help them grow. Most aspiring people want feedback, and the reason it may feel weird or unnatural is the fact that they do not receive it regularly. Thus, it feels strange.

Imagine the growth and development you can garner within your team if you just make a personal commitment (not a goal) to find a balanced and consistent approach to providing feedback. You can give positive and redirective feedback to your team at any time, and they just keep getting better. Imagine also the aura your will cast when you are seen and appreciated as a leader who teaches versus tells. A leader who people just want to work as hard as they can. A leader who is effective. The choice is simply yours to make.

You can always just go back to being a manager if you want.

CHAPTER SIX

Resilience
Learn How to Take a Left Hook

Life is simply difficult. Yet it can be filled with problems or opportunities. I tend to enjoy the optimist in me, so I find that I value both. However, within a retail store or a corporate office, you will and probably have already found that problems come in many different methods. From direct problems that hit you head-on to those darn sneaky ones, problems wiggle their way into your life no matter how awesome you may be. In this chapter, we are going to explore not just professional struggles but, more importantly, how to effectively deal with challenges and get back on your feet. For remember, you are a leader, and you have a team that is counting on you.

Imagine a typical day in a typical routine or meeting, and bam, a problem lands squarely on your lap. I mean, this one is pointing right to you, and it is looking like perhaps you screwed up. That feeling of blood rushing to your neck, and a bead of sweat is forming on your brow. Code red! Code red! Right? Potentially. Let's for a moment keep things in perspective. Assuming that you didn't do anything intentional, we can fix it. Let's add some gravity to this dilemma. Your boss was the kind soul that took the time to inform you of the problem, and she wants answers and a solution right away. What do you do? Oftentimes, it is a natural instinct to find the culprit, the person or process that created the issue. While it may quell nerves, it does nothing to fix the issue at hand. This is the iron-stomach moment where you must be the person to stand up and more than likely away from the group and take personal responsibility for the issue and ultimately take the right actions to fix the problem. Doesn't this sound rather simple? Yep. (I just answered this for you.) Too many times, we tend to be a zebra and try to blend into the crowd and find the dead man walking. This is not leadership. These are deflecting behaviors that are just plain wrong. An effective leader owns his or her problems equally to their success, period.

Yeah, you might have made a mistake. But imagine the shadow you will cast if you take personal responsibility. Imagine the silent micro messages you will send to your peers and your leader that you are the person that doesn't back down from a good ole-fashioned problem. Imagine if you fix it? You will more than likely receive an ample amount of praise for your leadership skills. Well, probably not directly, but you will live in the folklore of the office, store, or team. Someone around a campfire will be telling your story.

How does this have to do with resilience? Well, problems happen every day, and they should. That is why you have a job—to fix them. Let's dig a little deeper on this. Okay, so let's look at this two ways, and first, from a manager stance.

With managers, problems are often looked upon as interruptions to the task at hand. Even further, they are seen as a breakdown in the system or some weak-kneed person on a team that will have to go. The manager is drawn into problems as the fixer and the enforcer, right? Based on experience, this person has what it takes to insert one's self into the situation, analyze, fix (typically independently), and then find the cause of the problem and address. Sound like someone you know? Or have you been this person? Wait, are you this person? It is okay to be this person. Just get ready to pour sand on fires for the rest of your life. For you will probably have some serious upper-body strength!

Does the example above require resilience? Arguably not really. It takes persistence. It takes that hawk eye to ensure everything is going as prescribed. How boring! Hey, I am not knocking you, well, sort of. There are many jobs that require this type of management, and I appreciate that. However, this book is about leadership, so deal with it.

With leaders, problems are taken as an opportunity to teach and identify root-cause issues within the team dynamic. If there is a problem, oftentimes leaders stay at a professional distance to ensure the team gets into the resolution and offers coaching, advice, and support. Wait, this seems seriously hands-off, and isn't it our duty to get into the trenches and lead courageously to fix things? Short answer is no. Consider if you as the leader inject yourself too deeply within team problems, what would the intended and unintended consequences be? Would you stifle the creativity of individuals within your team? Yes. Would you overmanage those junior to you? Yes. Would you be teaching and training your team how to utilize effective critical thinking skills? No. Would your team be able to connect the dots of the problem, creative and critical thinking, varied attempts to identify root cause, and then ultimately find resolution to the problem? Nope, not even close.

A strong leader allows problems to occur. For they are golden opportunities for teams to learn resolution skills. Again, how can we tie in resilience here? The leader must have resilience to get past the ego of the problem's resolution. The leader must have the resilience to accept that problems will occur and understanding the same problem doesn't reoccur. This is excellent fodder for teams to grow. The leader must have resilience to understand that without problems, nothing great would come of anything. One of the best responses to a problem that lands in your team's lap is to ask your team, "What do you all propose we do to fix this now and in the long term?"

CHAPTER SEVEN

The Clopen
Finding the Energy

Your eyes are red, feet are sore, and you are gifted.

Ahhh, yes. The dreaded and most feared of all, the clopen. Some creative and drastically tired individual created this term of endearment. For you nonretail leaders, it's the lucky soul that gets the esteemed honor of closing a store at probably 10:00 p.m.–ish and then having the pleasure of being the opening manager the next very day. Now this doesn't sound like the end of the world, but I have a story to share of my personal and most lucky of lucky times in my career.

I was a store manager of a high-volume store, and it was roughly forty miles or so away from the ranch. A typical day was a ten-hour shift with an hour on each corner to get to and fro. Don't weep for me just yet. There are thousands of great people out there doing this day in and day out. I, again, am not special in any way. However, after a full and stressful day, the worst thing is to face another in a very short period of time.

So you arrive at work in the middle of the day, around eleven-ish. You kick butt all day long and even squeeze out a ten- or twenty-minute lunch. You are on your feet all day, making stressful decisions and looking at various issues that arise. You are tired, stressed out, and at times, even bored. Damn business is slow, and the sales plan doesn't change for that. The reason for this chapter is more humor than not, but this is a factual event that occurs every day. The way you can tell is by looking at the eyes of the manager you are dealing with. If they are short to make decisions, not really nice, and just want to fix the issue at hand, they are probably working on limited sleep, missing loved ones and family events, and drinking too much coffee. (Yeah, I just totally skipped around and had an out-loud distraction.)

Okay, back to story. So here I am trying to make a difference in my career and working hard for my team. I as the store manager personally chose to close every Friday to give my subordinate leaders the night off so they can take their loved ones out. Cool, huh? Yeah, you bet. Remember rule no. 4: totally do your best for your team and be selfless. I did this on my own. No one ever told me to. Just the right thing to do, by golly. I would let my team off a tad early on Fridays. So I would run the store alone from five to close. Now within a slower volume store, this isn't the worst thing in the world. However, in a cranker of a store, total sprint to the finish line full speed.

Imagine being the one to answer all the questions for five hours, getting change for registers, taking customer inquiries. Sounds rather easy, yes, but alone it's just tiring. (Again, I am not special here. I just find it important that you understand the dynamics of a day in the life.) This is also a special time, for as the store manager, you can bond with the team in a very cool way and get to know the team in an in-the-trenches fashion that you should be doing anyway. Also, based on performance, you can brag to your other managers that the good ole store manager can deliver a big day on their own! This time with the team is an honor. Don't forget about your role within your team. For they want to know you and how you got the position you have, the car your drive, the shoes you wear. Spending scheduled and consistent time with your team breeds trust, loyalty, and belief. All necessary ingredients to succeed.

It is roughly 11:30 p.m., and now I have an hour drive home. Get home just after midnight, and do you think it is possible to just go to sleep? Um, no. So you are probably hungry (horrible time of the night to eat). You watch some tube and then force yourself to go to bed at, say, 2:00 a.m.? Then you have to be at work at 6:00 a.m. or 7:00 a.m. Mine was 7:00 a.m. But I had to drop off my young son at my stepmother's home sixteen miles away. Let's do the math: going to bed at 2:00 a.m. plus getting up at 5:00 a.m. equals three hours of blissful, restful, harmonious sleep. Had to drop the lad and jet to the store. You feel like total crap and have to be a leader. This is an absolutely fantastic time to gut it out and show the team that you care enough as the senior leader to be selfless and be the role model of the dedication needed to lead. So you do all this, recover the store standards, lock the doors, and do all this in a matter of hours again. Thus, I give you the clopen.

Needless to say, I often think about these days and greatly respect the leaders that are subjected to this torture. The real question is why. Whilst the said schedule writer is scribing the schedule, don't they do the clopen scan? I mean, writing a leader schedule doesn't take a degree but more common sense and compassion. As a manager, it may be fair to say that if all shifts are covered, hours within budget, and designed to maximize efficiency, this is a good schedule. Yet as a leader, it goes beyond what I just described. A leader thinks about their team. The leader considers family, social events, baseball games, and guitar lessons. Surely the schedule must be maximized. However, giving the personal touch will keep the team's batteries charged, and they will give the leader their best only when the leader does the same.

I am not saying that being a leader means that they must bow to every request. It is about thinking about how to get the job done while giving your team a great work-life balance. Every once in a while, a clopen must occur, and when it does, a leader will have volunteers to do it. A manager simply schedules it. I hope you get what I am saying here. Take care of your team when it comes to the schedule. They may never tell you that they are upset or they feel like you do not consider their personal lives. The schedule is as close to their hearts as pay. For it has a direct impact on their lives and families. So next time you are shopping, check the eyes of the leader on duty. If they are red, ask them if they are enjoying a clopen. You will get a chuckle and most likely even better service.

CHAPTER EIGHT

Visitation
Take the Lead

In all positions within a retail store, at one point or another, you will interact with a company visitor. This is what is called a store visit. In this chapter, we will travel the lands and learn how to make a store visit awesome. Store visits are completed by a number of positions:

- Regional vice presidents—Typically in charge of a large territory such as Eastern US, Midwest, and West.
- District managers—Leads a number of stores within a smaller part of geography, works directly for RVPs, and leads store managers.
- Human resource managers—Leaders who assist the field leaders and teams to not make crazy decisions or do things even worse. (Always and I mean always treat your HR partner like a partner. They can and should be with you every step of the way.)
- Loss prevention managers—Leaders who think everyone is stealing. Really, they just do. Intrepid souls that have to deal with mystery and people who do, in fact, steal.
- Corporate visitors—These are the folks at the mother ship that work very hard mostly Monday–Friday and enjoy all the benefits of corporate life. Cubicles, meetings and holidays off. However, they are invaluable if you develop a

partnership. They are the special forces of their craft and can make things easy for you. Be nice and always welcome them to your store.

I have been visited and conducted thousands of store visits. There are a number of reasons why you will be visited. Let's explore.

A general store visit is usually conducted by a district manager, or DM. This visit consists of store standards, sales, and staff reviews. Occurs monthly or, for you outlying stores, quarterly. (For the extremely remote stores, annually. Lucky!) Store managers are expected to be on their toes with all aspects of their business. They typically will carry a binder of every report known to man about things they will never talk about. Here is how an example of how store managers get ready for a visit.

Ring, ring, ring. The telephone rings. Store leader answers, and it is the DM.

"Hey, Nic, how's it going?" asks the DM.

Nic, the store manager, or SM, responds with intrigue, "Great, ah, sir. How are you?"

"Listen, Nic, I am coming to visit you next Tuesday. I have some things I want to review with you."

Nic feels the stress enter his mind and gleefully responds, "Great. Is there anything I should prepare for?"

"No," responds the DM. "Just be ready to present your store, team, and business."

Now let's look at this exchange. Who was in charge? Yeah, the DM, right? Why? Clearly the DM can visit stores as they wish. However, did the store leader's reaction give you a sense of ownership or confidence? Hey, I get it. Visits can be grueling. They can be amazing too. The difference in my experience is not the cleanest store or even the best results. Rather, the leader that showcases their team and why the team is doing so well. This always makes visits for me fulfilling on both leaders.

I can always smell fresh paint, meaning a seasoned leader can immediately look for clues that just are not making sense. Typically, we all give extra spit and polish when we know company is coming.

However, when a store is too clean, my antenna raises. Let's examine some clues of fresh paint.

- Store managers that have every report known to the company and is just waiting for the DM to ask a question.
- Subordinate managers that have the same bundle of reports and are dizzy from quickly trying to memorize each report.
- Trailers behind the store. Yes, I once had a store manager that, when he knew the boss was coming, threw all discontinued, damaged, overstocked products on this trailer. When the DM visited, the store manager was praised for his excellent inventory management. (Role model material for sure.)

Always look at the eyes of the team when you arrive. If they are red, you know the team worked a ton of extra hours to get ready. Why is this a bad thing? Well, why did it take so much effort to get the store visit ready? And to that point, shouldn't the customer deserve the best? Sadly, too many times we give more effort to please a boss versus a customer. (We'll get to that in a few chapters. Hang tight for now.)

The actual reason for a store visit in my opinion is to teach the team how to do things better. I really do not know why leaders feel the need to inspect. Too many times I have endured long, boring, and contentious visits that accomplished absolutely nothing but to posture the leader for being such a "dynamic manager."

I do my best to make store visits fun and also challenging. I get nothing out of listening to myself, so I often ask as many questions as possible. There are some unspoken ground rules for you newer field leaders. And for the seasoned veterans, perk an ear up and read on.

Unspoken Store Visit Rules

1. *Be on time.* Everyone at the store you are visiting have been there for a while. (Even the closer came in early.) Show a sense of discipline and be there.

2. *Say hello to everyone that is working.* I mean a good face-to-face and handshake. Get to know the team. They are nervous as hell. Quell their fears with a smile and a question like "Have anything fun planned this summer?" Make it a point to leave the group of visitors when you see someone you do not know. This immediately shows a sense of interest in the team and sends a great message.

3. *Be authentic.* Do your best to teach the company way, but be careful not to be the smartest person on the visit. Or be cautious on the big words. We all know that Frank is loquacious, but honestly, Frank just likes to talk. Speak to your team and keep it real. Get me?

4. *Don't brag about your vast amounts of victories.* I often share more of my epic fails than wins with store leaders. For one, I actually failed and just do not want to see them repeat a bad move. We all know you are amazing. Stay humble, dude.

5. *Plan time for lunch!* I cannot for the life of me understand why so many people I have worked with find it an act of heroism for forgoing lunch. I find it completely unacceptable, and a midday respite is just what everyone needs. If you are doing an afternoon visit, be sure that the team has taken their lunch. They all will tell you, "Oh, don't worry, I'm not hungry." Make them eat. They need fuel, and again, imagine the amount of respect you garner if you actually care. I do not need fancy lunches, but a good thirty minutes of rest and a bite, and I am good to go for at least a couple more hours.

6. *Have a purpose for the visit.* Sometimes I drop in to say hello and see what I see. Most times, I have an audit or want to understand a business issue. For the preplanned full-store visits, I always send the team a calendar invite and let them know I am coming. This way, I can see how they prepare and know their business. Again, be on the lookout for fresh paint.

7. *Make visits fun.* It is physically and mentally possible to laugh and learn at the same time. Question is, do you want your team to describe you as their boss or leader? Bosses typically do not teach—they enforce. Leaders typically empower and inspire. The choice is yours. If the team hears you laughing, they will think the visit is going well. A somber, quiet tone gives shivers down their spine. Hey, if things are that bad and you cannot find anything to make light, you've got big problems on your hand. (Keep reading.)

8. *Connect observations to results.* Oftentimes, we let numbers do the talking. While mostly correct, it is important that you spend time just observing the team and their interactions. You can learn quite a bit from the team simply by watching.

9. *End with a teachable moment.* I find it important for the leader to recite what they took away from the visit. I want to hear it in their own words. Ensure they understand your intent, and boom, ready to roll.

10. *Thank the team for a good day.* Your team worked hard for you. Be sure to recognize it. I have always made it a practice to say goodbye to the entire team just as personal as I say hello.

In the end, your visits stay with your team. A famous quote from someone I have no idea who said, "People will forget what you said. People will forget what you did. However, they will never forget how you made them feel." Visit acumen takes time to get right. Be patient. No one really knows how great they should be. We all, though, know how bad they can be. Try to do your best, and if your team can say they are better because you were there, well, that is a great place to start.

> The grass ain't greener and the wine ain't
> sweeter on either side of the hill.
> —Jerry Garcia

CHAPTER NINE

Conference Calls Are an Evil Must, but Informal Meetings Are Better

Rule no. 3: Never take role on a conference call. It wastes time and costs a ton of payroll dollars annually. I want to illustrate this cost for you. So here I go, dang it.

You are the District Leader of fifteen stores for a large retailer. (Congrats on your promotion!) Okay, you just got off an important regional call, and you cannot wait to spread the word and invoke your first direction to your team. Each store has a store leader that earns a base salary of $60,000. This is roughly $32 per hour for each store leader. Multiply this by fifteen, and this equals to $480 per hour. For the nonstatistic types, hang with me here. It gets better. Even more detailed, you are paying $8 per minute each time you have a call.

Okay, so you schedule a call for 1:00 p.m., and being an eager and impatient person, you activate your call a couple minutes early to show urgency. For some reason, as adults, we feel the need to take a roll call. You begin your call, and you hear the normal beeps as your team joins the call. You have fifteen stores, so it takes a couple of minutes to crank out the roll call. (I am violently against roll call, even worse when the leader doesn't use the names of their team members but just the store numbers. How out of touch while doing something so painful.)

12:58 p.m.

"Bill from 1436?"

"Here, sir."

"Sally from 1658?" Crickets. "Sally?" *Beep.* "Sally? Who just joined?"

"Me."

"Who is that?"

"Terry from 1241."

"Oh, okay, Hello Terry. Sally? Will someone shoot a text to Sally, please? James from 1314?"

Garbled response, "Which James?"

"From 1314."

Nothing.

1:02 p.m.

"Sally is here! Hello? Did you call my name yet?"

"Hi, Sally, I did."

"Sorry I was late. I was helping a customer."

"Okay, no problem, and thanks for joining."

"You bet! We are busy today, and I had a customer that needed help with a new product. Guess what?"

"What, Sally?"

"I sold it! Yep, did it all by myself, and my team is very excited."

"Good to hear that."

"Thanks! Did you get my e-mail yesterday regarding the broken toilet?"

"Sally, can I give you a call after this call to talk about it?"

"Uh, okay. Just didn't want you to forget about my broken toilet."

"I didn't, and we can talk about the toilet after this call, Sally."

"Okay, thanks. So what is this call about?"

"Sally, I am taking roll and will share with the team in just a minute."

"Okay, thanks."

1:06 p.m.

"Aiden from 1575? Aiden from 1575? Aiden? Will someone—"

"I'm here! Sorry, I was on mute. I was answering you each time! Just realized I was on mute!"

"No worries, Aiden, and thanks. Say, gang, please do not stay on mute. I like for us to be able to participate."

Loud phone ringing in the background and continues to ring.

"Will someone either answer the other phone or put themselves on mute, please?"

"Sorry," says Sally. "My cordless was ringing."

"We can hear that, Sally."

"I am going to go on mute."

"Okay."

1:19 p.m.

The district leader finishes roll call at approximately 1:19 p.m. Let's do some math here. From 12:58 p.m. to 1:19 p.m., the district leader completely wasted time and showed a tremendous lack of control. The punctual leaders had to sit through the misery of it all. The quiet and disengaged leaders really didn't care, and the, we'll say, lower-performing leaders made roll call hell. This is twenty-one minutes at a rate of $8 per minute, so that was $168 in labor expense to destroy a good day and erode profitability. If you are a regional leader and oversee a market of twelve district leaders that behave in a similar manner, this would have just cost you $2,016. From a company perspective, if there are four regional leaders that oversee sixty-two district leaders, this would cost the company weekly $10,416, and to annualize this expense, it costs $541,632 to take a roll call!

Consider the expense at all levels of your organization. Plainly put, unless there is a sensitive issue or a mandatory must, roll call is just frivolous. Trust your leaders to attend. If you fear that they are not on the call, you have bigger issues. Your team is full of great people that do not need to be treated anything other than awesome.

As the more teams I lead in my life so far, the better at calls I have become. Trust me, I used to listen to other leaders and try to mimic their style. It never really felt genuine to me, so I was either foolish or daring and started to do them my way. I didn't take roll call, only had a few things I wanted to cover, and empowered my team to do the majority of the talking. I used captains of certain parts of the business. I would ask a store leader that had a particular passion for a part of the business to own it for the team and help shepherd the team along. This way, I was giving away the autocratic control from myself and empowering a leader to do what they supposed to do—lead. I would start my calls with the traditional "Hey, gang," ask how everyone is doing, and review big rocks of what I needed to cover. Less than fifteen minutes from me and then on to the captains! Each captain would speak to their part of the business, share best practices, and get the team working together. The real win here is that the more the team worked together, the better the results. Oh, I was able to simply add value only when appropriate and do this very rare thing called listen.

In today's retail environment, cost control is huge. Meetings are generally not a good idea to avoid travel and expense. I appreciate this idea when it comes to national meetings. I hate these! Lots of coworkers trying to outdo one another and posture for face time with the bosses. This reminds me of a true and, say again true, story.

Story time. I was in Las Vegas, Nevada, for a national meeting. I had just been promoted to district manager. The meetings were about the upcoming holiday and how we as an organization were going to do what had never been done before. Anyway, as I have said, not the biggest fan of meetings. Well, in those days, I had to share a room with another district manager. (Totally creepy, if you ask me. If we didn't take roll call on conference calls, we would have the money to spring for separate rooms.)

The meeting ended for the day, and we all ate our communal dinner and then go to, you guessed it, the bar. I had a drink with my mates and retired early to grab some sleep. I didn't want to be awake when a total stranger was going to bed next to me. Let me clarify, I had one drink and bolted to my shared room. Sharing a bit of personal information here, I sleep in a shirt and boxers. That's how I have done it for years. (This is an important detail for the story. I'm not being weird.)

I drifted off to sleep like any other night, and I was suddenly woken up by hitting my head on something. I opened my eyes and found myself outside of my room, standing in the hallway of a very large and expensive hotel. Wait a minute, where in the hell am I? I forgot to mention that, at times, I have been known to sleepwalk. OMG, I am in my delicates, in a hallway of a hotel that my entire team and boss is staying! Code red! Code red! Dive! Dive! Dive! I immediately found my room, and I did not have my key, of course. What was I going to do?

I then heard voices getting off the elevator, and they were coming my way. I couldn't be the new district manager that was caught in his undies! I scanned the hallway and saw a custodial room. I ran to that, and the door opened! "Phone? Please? God, help me?" No. There was a service elevator though. I hit the button, the door opened, and I hid in this elevator. I figured I could use this to recon each floor for a phone, security guard, or Jesus himself. I visited each floor until a very nice lady was waiting to get on the service elevator. She looked me up and down, rolled her eyes, and stood next to me on the elevator. I asked her if she had a phone, and she simply replied, "No." Strike two. I went down to another floor, and bam, I saw a phone. I grabbed it (in my underwear) and called the operator. I asked if they could send a security guard to my room to let me in.

They responded, "Yes, sir, but you will need to come to the front desk to identify yourself."

I responded, "I am unable to do that, and I am requesting an urgent need for security."

"Why, sir?"

"Well, I just need security, please and thank you."

"Okay, sir, you will need to prove your identity prior to being let in."

"I am unable to do that prior for I do not have my wallet on me at this very moment."

"Okay, sir, well, it will be twenty to thirty minutes for we are very busy with a company meeting."

"I know, I am part of the company that is here."

I returned to the elevator and went back up to my floor to wait the longest twenty to thirty minutes of my life. I hid in a very, very small closet, and I could see the hallway. I saw a number of my peers and subordinate leaders walking back to their rooms in a drunken and jovial state. Just imagine if they saw me? Would I be fired for being a super creep? I think I made actual eye contact with someone. Well, time passed, my heart continued to race, and my pulse was going one hundred miles per hour! I then saw the angelic security guard. I burst from the closet in a manner that must have scared the crap out of this old security guard. He looked me up and down and asked, "Young man, where are your clothes? I am going to call the police."

"Sir, I can explain. I work for the company that is meeting here, and I simply was sleepwalking. That's it."

Giving me an unsure look, he asked for my ID. "Sir, do you think I have my wallet? I can show you my ID when you let me in the room."

Just then I heard the voice of my boss.

"Sir, I am in a real pinch here! I really do not need to be standing in this hallway, in my undies, with people getting off the elevator! Please!"

"This is going to be a good story for my boys in security, but okay."

He let me in. I showed my ID and politely slammed the door. I let out a sigh, no, scream of relief that I was able to get back into my room unseen. I mean, James Bond himself would have probably been proud. Just then the door opened again, and it was my roommate. I knew him and shared what had just happened, stupidly in detail. He just laughed at me and went to bed. I did make him promise not to tell anyone.

In the morning, we all assembled for breakfast, and I had this weird feeling that everyone in the room, all four hundred of them, knew of my tribulations. No one said anything, and we all then filed into the general meeting room. My boss opened the meeting with a story of a complaint that was received the night before of a certain district manager wearing Brooks Brother and alligator boxers wandering the halls and if any of us knew anything about this. Right then I gave the hundred-mile stare to my roommate, who was laughing his ass off.

My boss called my name and said, "Mr. Travilla, would you know anything about this?"

I stood and said, "Nope."

My boss jokingly said, "Come on, tell us a story, Mr. Travilla."

The whole room erupted with laughter, and I did. I told my story in vivid detail, and in the end, it brought me closer to the team. Still hear about those cool boxers to this day.

Big picture, we all make mistakes. Own them and laugh it off if you can. So what does this have to do with conference calls? Nothing. Just a funny story if you ask me. Let's get back to conference calls. They are horrible. They are impersonal, and big picture, people can hide like a zebra on them.

In my years, I have witnessed many different types of calls. Ones that have provided simple information and ones that have lit the fires of hell and gotten a team to do the impossible. What is the difference? The two different examples require a phone and a group of people to call a number and say, "Here." (Hope you got that dig at roll call. The fact that I just gave it away probably just killed the humor. Oh, well, I tried.) In reality, the difference is the leader. Either the leader sets the tone and nurtures a good discussion, or perhaps a manager downloads information and reads PowerPoint slides. Have you endured anything like this yourself? I am sure you and have and most likely do on a basis.

Imagine if you as the leader took brave step, and instead of a weekly call, you chose to layer in an in-person meeting each month. What benefits do you feel you could garner if you just cut a callout and had a gathering of your team? I know what you are thinking. "Well, no one else on my team does that" or "It is too expensive to get everyone together." That paradigm will be certain doom if you as the leader do not have the courage to go outside of the box. Be bold!

Do something different for a change. Your team will thank you. Oh, and don't have a packed agenda either. Cover just a few important things, and a tip is to give your team the empowerment for them to create the agenda. Yes, you can cover what you must, but team synergies will make the meeting one they will not forget. And by adding this, empowerment has duality in accountability for participation too. So let's recap. This is an important learning, and I want to ensure there is alignment on not just how but, even more important, why.

- Conference calls are totally painful. Even the best ones are just so impersonal.
- Never ever, ever take roll call (unless required by law.)
- Ensure you ask lots of questions to get the team talking versus listening. (Please don't be the smartest person on your call. Your title alone garners respect.)
- Keep them short. My rule is an hour. Yours can be different, but it is difficult to keep the ball rolling much past an hour.
- Be on time to your own call.
- Stick to the agenda. Sidebars destroy continuity.
- Laugh if you can and smile when you speak. Your team can see and feel your tone through the call.
- Don't try to solve everything on the call. Things can be fluid. It's okay.

Well, good luck on your next call. I am sure you will try some of these amazing techniques and most likely screw up. That's okay too. Being human is a great attribute of a leader.

CHAPTER TEN

Meeting Etiquette
Staying Just Long Enough

Should I stay or should I go?
—The Clash

Oh, boy. This chapter is going to be a doozy. I just got done telling to have meetings with your team, right? Well, get ready because I am going to get deeper into your behavior during meetings and how to lead effectively through them. I am going to focus more on being an attendee versus the one giving the meeting, but will touch on both.

Meetings must happen. Proven fact. They are designed to get a bunch of people together to work things out toward a solution. They also can be dynamic for two opposing forces can often find common ground. Oftentimes when in said meeting, you will find others staring at their phones, having a sidebar discussion, and generally not being present. This begs the question as to why have the meeting in the first place if no one is going to participate.

Being a leader, you will give and participate in a number of meetings both formal and informal. A key ingredient for success is when you are there, be there. Your time is the single most precious resource you have, and you must use it wisely. There are no points for how many meetings you may have stacked on your calendar but rather the contributions you give when you are in the meeting.

Have you ever met someone that tells you that they are too busy to talk because they are going to a meeting? I very much believe that many coworkers find solace in meetings. Why? Because it fills their calendar. It gives them things to do or, more accurately, somewhere to be. It can be a reason to miss a deadline, make a difficult decision, and actually do their job. Meetings are like mini vacations from accountability. When there are a bunch of people in a room, oftentimes the spotlight has trouble finding them.

Think about your typical work schedule. If you are a store team member, you will most likely have a daily pep rally or morning kick-off meeting. These are actually fun and a good way to get the mojo going for the day. The Walmart leaders of the glory years in the early eighties started each day with a huge hand-clapping, song-singing pep rally. Employee loyalty and engagement were through the roof, as were their sales and profits. While I never had the opportunity to attend one of these beauties, I can only imagine the fun factor. Motivating a team member that is earning close to minimum wage isn't easy, but with heart and soul, it is possible. Being a store manager myself, I had the privilege to host hundreds of morning kickoff meetings. They started out horrible. I would get on the PA and call everyone to the front of the store and review numbers and things to do for the day. I even worked for a company that required a thirty-minute training seven days per week. Anyone caught not doing the mandatory training would nearly be shot on sight.

As I matured into role, I found that my teams were less focused on results but more on one another. They wanted to celebrate birthdays and small accomplishments and even talk some good smack toward one another. (You know, who is going to beat whom in sales.) The more I harnessed the teams' energies, the more I was connecting with them. The more I connected with them, the more they would listen to me when I asked of them. See how this evolution starts? Get away from just the business, and talk to with your team versus at them. No one really cares about store rankings (except you). If all you talk about are things that matter solely to store leaders, then you are missing 99 percent of the team. If you start every meeting with numbers and results, you are most likely boring the hell out of your team. If you use the pronoun *I* in your meeting, you are going to lose your team. Meetings are about *us*. What is important to the team must be performance. However, there are lots of great ways to lead your team to the promised land.

There is an old adage, "People believe what they say, not what you say." Sounds true, but how the heck do you even approach this phrase? Well, pretty simple if you think about it. Ask questions, right? Consider if you started meetings off with questions. What do you think you would hear? Most likely the sweet sounds of crickets chirping. Why? Because people are used to listening and enduring meetings versus actively participating. Leaders often feel compelled to lead, and this for some reason gives them the sense that they must do all the talking. Guess the learning here can be leaders can lead while others are leading. It is fantastic to let go and let your team lead.

Trust me, when it is time for you to take the reins, you will. And your team will recognize this and appreciate you stepping in. So I want you to pinky promise me that the next time you feel the need to have a meeting, let your team take a big part of it, and you might just be amazed to see just how great they really are.

CHAPTER ELEVEN

Why a Good Pair of Shoes Can Change Everything

This chapter is dedicated to all the amazing people that work on their feet day in and day out. You are warriors. Don't let nobody tell you anything else.

Shoes are a must for those in the workplace. Well, retail workplace, that is. Those free-spirited folks in different vocations fit right in sans shoes. I remember my very first pair of dress shoes I purchased for my days as a paint mixer at the large department store. I think I got them from J. C. Penney. They were burgundy, slip-on, wing-tipped loafers. I looked more like a gangster versus an associate earning a robust $4.50 per hour. I mean, I would wear these everywhere. Days off, it didn't matter. I loved them. I would often tell my friends I was a businessman and I just had to wear them. Picture this, in shorts and a T-shirt, I sported these kicks everywhere.

So why would I include a chapter about shoes in a leadership book? Easy answer, they are critical to your success. In fact, I tend to examine not only what type of shoe a person is wearing but, a tad more importantly, how they maintain their shoes. (I do not have a shoe fetish, I promise, but details matter.)

Let me be clear: You do not need to own expensive shoes. You simply need to take care of your shoes. How? Here you go. (I should have a Marine drill instructor review this prior, but I do not want to do any push-ups right now.)

Rule 1: Do not wear the same pair of shoes every day. Your kicks need to rest just like you. Wearing them every day is certain doom for them under one year. Your feet sweat in shoes, and the salt erodes the leather. Having a second go-to pair of shoes will give you the rotation you need.

Rule 2: Never put your shoes on in the dark. I did this one early and groggy morning only to find out that I had two completely different shoes on. Oh, and I was traveling, so I had the pleasure of this dynamic screwup all day. To be clear, I was wearing one black shoe and one brown shoe all damn day. I had to explain this far too often from morning to night.

Rule 3: This is a critical step that I will credit my father, Gregg, or to his peeps, Muggs, for his tutelage. Every time you purchase a pair of shoes, make sure you purchase shoe trees. These are wooden inserts that do amazing things. They keep the shape of your shoe, they are made of cedar and smell far better than your feet, and finally, they help remove the sweat and salt from your shoes.

Rule 4: Clean your shoes as needed, but at least monthly. You can buy a kit from any shoe store. The kit will contain the following:

- Black shoe polish. (Spring for the parade gloss polish. It gives a better luster.)
- Horse hairbrush. This is what you use to clean dust and to remove the polish.
- Edge dressing. Black liquid to apply to the outer edge of your sole.

Rule 5: When in an airport, always get a professional shoe shine. These rare and, in recent times, lonely professionals will make you look like a champ. They really know how to get your shoes in order. Don't be a cheapskate and get a beer at a bar over a shoeshine.

I am not going to get into how to polish your shoes. You can YouTube that. Just make sure you pay attention to the health and look of your shoes. Some common areas to look at are the following:

- *The heel of your shoes.* These wear out the fastest, and if you do not bring them to a cobbler for replacement, you will wear down the wooden part of your shoes. Spend the forty dollars a couple of times a year to get your heels replaced.
- *Soles.* Based on usage and where you work, these wear out slower but most definitely wear out. If your feet get wet when you step in a puddle, time to see the cobbler.

Using shoe trees and rotating will prolong the life of your shoes. Personally I prefer leather-bottomed soles, but they can get your dogs barking early in the day if you are on your feet. The good ole rubber-soled shoes do just fine for the more competitive types.

Really do not want to get into styles or brands, but you most certainly get what you pay for when it comes to shoes. Not saying that you need to rush out and pay four hundred dollars for Italian loafers, but getting a solid pair or two is a must for a leader. I shall not give any credit to brands. However, there is a very good shoe company based in Wisconsin that makes a wonderful pair of shoes.

Okay, lots of talk about shoes. You will thank me if you follow these steps and just make it part of your routine. That next promotion might be a result of those swank kicks you wore at your last meeting! (Probably not, but it sounded good when I wrote it.)

CHAPTER TWELVE

Balancing and Not Balancing Your Family

Pay attention here. I am not a pro at this at all. However, I do work on this every day. I don't know what great looks like, but I sincerely love my family both far and near.

Leaders work long hours and show a tremendous amount of selflessness when it comes to the schedule. At times, the situation will call for leaders to roll their sleeves up and get it done. Also, there are times when the workload will ease for a breather. This is the window we as leaders must recognize, try to plan for, and spend time away. No matter your position, we all need rest. We are not robots and cannot sustain perfection without a break. Wait, no one is perfect, so don't even try.

Work-life balance at work is sold and marketed as a benefit. Should this really be a benefit? If a company feels the need to purvey this as a benefit, I can only imagine what every day may be like. This speaks more to culture versus a benefit. It is called work because it requires work to get it done. A lack of balance with work and too much life would certainly not garner intended results. So it is up to the leader to make the right call, meaning when to say when. Highly subjective, right?

I know you at one point in your career, or even last week, felt the sting of trying to balance family obligations and something at work. We all have. So let's talk about some situations and possible solutions to get the right critical thinking going.

For example, you are a retail leader working your way up the ladder within the store, let's say a department manager. The company requires two closes and two full weekends per month. (Personally I don't understand why companies do this. Let the store leader make the decision with good partnering and oversight.) Nonetheless, you bow to the wishes of senior leaders or, for that, managers. You are a loyal soul and work your required schedule. However, one week, you have some family coming to visit for a graduation and another is a graduation party.

There is a large sale going on this month that has the whole company excited. There are e-mails, conference calls, memos, and you were even graced with a district visit too. I'm talking big sale! Your store leader is running around telling everyone that this sale will be bigger than Black Friday. You too get excited to move some inventory and perhaps carve out a good quarterly bonus.

During a weekly leadership meeting, the store leader explains that for this month, the team is required to work every weekend to maximize coverage and drive sales. Yet there is one small caveat. Your store leader explains that he will be away for one full weekend due to plans he couldn't change and casually says, "This is why I have a solid management team. I know you all will do a great job!"

Your heart sinks. Sweat beads on your brow. Your pulse races. You immediately start thinking how you will tell your husband about your schedule. (Your schedule is already a point of contention within your marriage because your husband is a teacher.)

Without any questions, your store leader adjourns the meeting, and you and your fellow department leaders just look at one another. Nothing is said, but the body language alone is telling a story of disengagement. After the initial shock, you get the courage to find your store leader. You politely explain that you too have plans that you are unable to miss. You go into detail regarding the family that is traveling quite a distance to visit and the large family party the following weekend. In addition, you also mention that you typically never take the two full weekends off anyway, yet these two are very important to you and your family.

Quickly your store leader looks at you indifferently and simply says, "This is what corporate wants. It is not my direction, sorry." You boldly and with a racing pulse say, "I understand. However, there was no notice, and I wonder how you were able to take a weekend off?" The look of indifference from your store leader now changes to defensive anger. "Because I am the store leader and I have worked very hard to have power over my schedule. It isn't appropriate to question me."

What do you do?

You have a number of options. Let's choose our own adventure.

Option A: You can simply accept the direction of corporate leaders and the fact that your store leader, in some way, worked his way up and earned flexibility. Work the weekends and deal with your family on your own time. You will most likely fight day and night with your husband, but hey, you too are working your way up the ladder so it is worth it.

Option B: You politely push back on your store leader and explain that you are never the manager that complains and these two weekends are super important and you are just as important as he. You ask him to reconsider or at least give some thought to your request. You even suggest partnering with the district leader or human resources. You get a look of disloyalty and frustration from your store leader, and nothing else is said.

Option C: You put your foot down and state that this is just not fair and that you will have to take this issue to human resources. You haven't really enjoyed your position and have just dealt with it for hopes of a promotion to another store. At this point, you feel there is nothing to lose. Your store leader is furious and walks away.

Is there an outcome that feels right? Within each of these scenarios, you are on the losing side. From the hope that your store leader will change his mind to outright protest, you just picked the short straw. Yet too many times, I firmly believe this happens to a significant amount of subordinate leaders. Should we just accept this? Or is there a better manner in which to approach work-life balance?

The answer: solid maybe!

Exploring the root cause to this scenario speaks to the fact that the subordinate leader failed to notify her store leader and assumed that nothing would change. When it did, the leader freaked out (rightfully so) and went into damage control, yet most likely caused more damage both professionally and personally. In my days as a store leader, I was this guy. In my early days, I would take the best days off and work the schedule I "deserved." I quickly learned that my entire team was plotting my slow demise.

The schedule is as sensitive as pay for most working folks. It has a direct effect on, well, everything. The key here is to communicate. And I mean communicate! Not the day before, but there should be a strategic system for leaders to communicate important dates to work and not to work. I learned that a master calendar in my office worked for me. My leaders would populate dates well in advance, and in most cases, I was able to take care of them. There will always be times when you as the senior leader must say no. However, pending those times are few, your team will get it. Also (listen up here) there are times too when you as the senior leader needs to break the rules and take care of your team. Now I am not talking about reckless and play-by-your-own rules behavior. I am talking about making a call for the betterment of your team and their family. This takes critical thinking, guts, experience, failure, lessons learned, and a will to be a caring leader.

In this scenario, what would you have done if you were the store leader? There is risk: if you take care of one, you might be held accountable to take care of the entire team. Then you are getting off the rails big-time. District leaders tend to freak out if you as the store leader make your own rules.

Let's consider some better options in this scenario. During the meeting, if you remember, the store leader dropped the bomb that all weekends were cancelled due to the big sale, right? Yet he did manage to surgically insert his time off. Consider these options:

Option A: "Gang, have some news from the corporate leaders. We have a very exciting sale starting next week. I just received direction that the normal weekend off rotation is on hold to support this sale. Now, I know you have lives and plans. Does this impact anyone here? If so, how can we band together and make it work?"

This is a Socratic approach to help the team understand the importance and to respect time off. You will need a solid team here. For I have tried this approach, and if you have a selfish team that doesn't work well together, you will get a bunch of blank stares and arms crossed. They will not want to help one another out. You will have to be the boss here and make a decision.

Option B: Store leader explains the sale and working requirements. "I just reviewed the time-off calendar and see that you, Stephanie, have some very important days with your kids and family. You know, gang, that I want to follow the rules, but graduations happen just once. Is there any flexibility in your plans, Steph, and is anyone able to help Stephanie out?"

This is the people's champion approach that can work out well with a great team that values one another. Typically, a team like this will work it out for themselves. Also, the leader that needs the time off will more likely be flexible because she cares about her team too. (Pure nirvana.)

Option C: Store leader explains the sale and working requirements. "We are far from corporate. I don't see the need to take all your weekends away. I will still give you all a weekend day off, and we will need to keep this quiet. I will have you on the schedule, but you can take the day off. We should be fine. I really like you all and want you to be happy at work."

Completely wrong. You immediately lose credibility as a leader being the nice guy. While your team will appreciate the time off, good leaders will have a weird feeling in their gut for going against the grain. Your leaders will lose trust in you.

The learning here should be that, at times, you will be faced with tough decisions that clearly make an impact your team's lives. As the leader, you are always on stage to do things correctly. That is, for the sake of your team and the business. As is with most things in life, a solid process can reduce the need to break rules. Remember, your team is devoted to you as their leader, and you must, and I repeat must, show a strong sense of discipline and compassion. One must not outweigh the other. And this takes time to hone your skills. In the end, taking care of your team in a responsible manner will earn the trust and respect of your team to walk through the fires of hell for you. Anything else is a quick way to fail.

When it comes to work-life balance, I have never met a person that has this dialed in perfectly. Life happens, and you as the leader must react. Keeping your family at the center of decisions is a good start. Remember, your job and coworkers do not tuck you in at night. Nor do your kids pay the bills. Balance, just go for balance.

CHAPTER THIRTEEN

1:1s
They Really Mean a Lot to Your Team

Time is a created thing. To say "I don't have
time" is like saying "I don't want to."
—Lao Tzu

Scheduling time for anyone is a gift. As a leader, you will be judged upon how you spent your time. This sentence gives the sense that time is allocated like money. You spend both time and money in a similar mental process. The overly used phrase "I am busy" is probably the worst thing you can do to your team. For we are all busy. No one is busier than anyone. People just allocate their time differently.

One-on-ones, statuses, touch bases, face times, they all give your focus to someone else. These are time blocks dedicated to reviewing business, development, dreaded annual reviews, and such. Yet we all have a calendar, right? Why don't more people schedule these with their teams more often? Is it the constant craving of doing more that gets us away from developing our teams? In this chapter, we will explore why you as a leader must, and I say again must, schedule time for your leaders. The greatness that can be built, the skills that can be harnessed, and the results you can achieve can all be accomplished by listening.

In my experience, I have only had a handful of bosses that took time for me via a scheduled 1:1. The first time I attended, I had nearly every report the company provided sitting in alphabetical order. I clamored through each metric to ensure that I was able answer any question possible regarding my sales trends, my costs of goods, my EBIDTA, and even my line items with shrink. I mean, I studied and studied! This was a phone 1:1 with a regional vice president. I was looking at the clock tick away down to my scheduled time. Sweat beading, fingers tapping, heart pounding. "The time is now! My 1:1 is here!" Waiting for phone to ring. Still waiting for phone to ring. "Maybe I needed to call him?" I asked. "Crap! I am late! I am going to call, but the invite said he was calling me!" The agony! *Ring!* Two minutes over my scheduled time, the phone rang. "Brian Travilla, may I help you?" (Seriously? Did I just answer the phone that way?)

My boss replied, "Hey, Brian! What's up?"

"Oh, eh . . . nothing, sir, just ready to talk about my sales, profit, inventory, team, shrink, and well, eh . . . anything else you want to know about my business."

"Okay, how about we start about you. How are you doing?" my boss replied in a warm and subtle tone.

The only thing I didn't prepare for was me. I was stumped! I simply replied, "Fine, been very busy trying to improve sales within a few stores, but I foresee positive growth due to some new leaders I have hired."

"Dude, I mean . . . you. How are you? And how is your family?" (What? Why does he want to know about me and my family?)

We spent the fastest hour of my life not talking about business at all. We spoke about my family, my boys' baseball, and his daughter going to college soon. Then it went to where I was planning my family vacation. We touched on a few business questions, and his response was "I am not worried at all. I believe in you, Brian. You'll fix it, I know."

So there I was. In total awe. My first 1:1 with a regional vice president, and it went completely different that I would have ever thought. I felt like I was valued. I felt engaged. I felt cared about. And I was 100 percent determined to kick some serious tail in leading my team to a no. 1 ranking within the company. (Self-glorifying addition here, we did finish no. 1 that year. Great job, team!)

A few questions hit me pretty hard though.

1. Why didn't we do the deep dive into my business?
2. Did he take it easy on me for some reason?
3. Did he detect I wasn't ready to explain my business?

All the questions were stemming from being insecure and inexperienced in business relationships. I had learned that not every discussion needs to be business. There are indeed other topics in life that matter too. We had monthly 1:1s from there for about a year and a half. They were usually a few minutes late, and at times, we did dig into the nuts and bolts. However, this was time that my boss always stressed was my time. It was up to me to lead the conversation. This increased my business acumen tremendously. It also held me accountable to come to the meeting with substance to share versus listen to a litany of questions and download. I was nearly starstruck that a leader so talented as this gave me an hour of his time each month.

Fast-forward a few months, and like any good leader, I copied his approach with my team. (Yeah, stole his mojo.) I had recently taken over a new district that comprised stores from three different districts and combined them into one. This was exciting. However, there was quite a bit of work to do to set my expectations and also work out the kinks of "My former DM did it this way."

Oftentimes, store leaders do not use the calendar function as field leaders do. Well, I sent each store leader a personalized invite for a monthly reoccurring 1:1. I was purposely vague as to what to prepare. I wanted to gauge the critical thinking of my team and see what they would bring to the meeting. What I experienced was similar to my level of neurotic preparation to just showing up.

Big picture, this method allowed me time with each leader and to connect, engage, and set the right environment of learning. Yep, I just stressed learning. For remember, we as leaders are teachers. Our job is to make others better. During these 1:1s, I found that this was a fantastic way to get to know my team, what drives them, their hobbies, and their dreams. This sounds grandiose, I know. However, scheduling open time for each team member created a relationship of trust, belief, and gut-felt loyalty to the team.

It is important to stress here that the magic doesn't just happen because you both show up. It takes few key things:

- The leader must be willing to allow unstructured time. No long action lists. Follow up or touch basing on a few things is fine. But the creativity that can be produced from a less-is-more approach may just surprise you. (Allow it to unfold.)
- The leader should describe the environment as risk-free and dedicated to the subordinate. An opening statement that I find that works well is "How is everything going?" or "Share with me what's moving and shaking" and even "How was your day off yesterday? Do anything fun?"
- The subordinate must understand that this is an evolving process and nothing ever goes 100 percent to plan. Together, the leader and subordinate can hammer out a meaningful and productive 1:1.
- At the conclusion, the main learning shouldn't be sports or just fun stuff but topics that blend in business, personal, and development. There should be a commitment from both parties on how they will work hard for each other. No one-way commitments!

Overall, the goal here is to learn the value of prioritizing time for you and your team to share, communicate, and grow together. If you have never been on the receiving end of a productive 1:1, I feel for you. However, just because you haven't doesn't mean you can change that for your team today. Also, I encourage you to manage upward and share this chapter with your boss. Be cautious, but lead with courage and help them out. They may have read this book. Yet. okay, you are now ready to boil the ocean with the learning adventure! Whatever you do, don't start this and get busy and only get this going for a few rounds. If you stumble, hold yourself accountable and get back in the game. Your team will appreciate your discipline and dedication. If not, your team will not forget your lack of dedication and reward you with turnover and poor results.

In a few months from now, read this chapter again. Imagine how excited you are going to be when you are the 1:1 ninja. I'll bet you have learned things about your team that you may not have ever thought. Also, I'll also bet you will be feeling quite a bit more in control of your business than before too. Hmmmm, sounds pretty cool, eh?

CHAPTER FOURTEEN

Physical and Spiritual Work
It's Work, so Work

I am a Deadhead. I play the guitar in a Dead tribute band. I jog in nature. I believe in earthly energy. These things in my life mean quite a bit to me. No, I do not think I am a hippie. Well, perhaps a modern-day person that believes in peace, love, and happiness.

I have also been a person devoid of happiness and just worked a ton. Every day was a grinder without a compass. No music, no rusty strings on a guitar, no band, little to no nature, and deaf to natures energy. Why? I had a lack of balance in my life and was on the treadmill of personal failure. Yes, job was doing well, making my sales plans, earning bonuses, but I was goddamn miserable. (Oh, I gained about forty-five pounds too.)

So why the polar examples? Because it happens. This negative lifestyle wasn't an overt choice but a combination of a bunch of bad decisions. How do you feel when you read *physical and spiritual work*? I'll bet some of you are thinking church pews and the gym, right? Well, for some leaders, this is exactly the right choice. For others, it can be completely different. The key here is to find what drives you and what fills your gas tank.

Personally, I love to jog and jog for hours. My wife, Charlene, isn't the largest fan, for I often complain of, well, every joint aching. For me, it is a release of stress and pressure. While I love the Dead,

I never listen to music when I run because I love to hear the birds, trees, and wind blowing.

A bit of how I found the gumption to lose the forty-five pounds and get my butt in gear. Hey, I am not grandstanding, but it was work, and I mean work! I looked at a picture of me holding my first son, Nicolas, and saw two of me. I was embarrassed and couldn't believe it. However, when you eat fast food, work sixty to seventy hours per week, and drink energy drinks all day, should I have expected anything else? Add in the stress and grief of losing my father, Gregg, right before Nicolas was born. It was just a difficult period of my life. Yes, these are all excuses, but I am human too.

In my early twenties, I was a big runner and was in great shape. Working a million hours a week and not caring about what I ate didn't have the negative effects that when you get a bit older. During this time, I was a machine. Sleep was overrated, and work was fun.

Back to unhealthy Brian. I was a store director for a large company, and the pressure was significant on a daily basis. I felt at that time that working more hours was the answer to soft sales and margin compression. Eating whenever I could and, well, as much as I could would often stem the pressure for a few minutes of relief. The dollar menu at any fast-food joint was my friend. Chugging caffeine, eating burgers, and a donut or two on Sundays was my coping mechanism. Boy, did I forget about all the things that I loved. It was just a daily grind to not totally suck. Well, this went on for about a year, and I was 100 percent miserable. The commute, pressure, lack of success, unhealthy appearance, unhealthy overall, and just a complete negative attitude, I was done.

I looked in the mirror and found that I had lost myself to a job and was behaving totally out of control. I was driving home around midnight, and the thought of me jogging again ran through my mind. (Literally yes.) I was starving and would make my usual stop and grab a burger. I said, "Not tonight." I knew it wasn't good for me, and why was I even thinking about this? Routines and habits, that's why. I kept driving until I went home. My wife, Charlene, is a possible vampire. (For she doesn't believe in going to bed anytime before 2:00 a.m. Weird, I know. Perhaps in another book.) I asked my wife what was wrong with me.

She replied gently, "Oh, what do you mean?"

"Really?" I said. "Look at me. I am never happy and always on the verge of losing it. Look at my gut!"

"I love you no matter," she said.

I thanked her, but her acceptance wasn't good enough for me "Going Down the Road Feeling Bad" (amazing Grateful Dead tune).

I went to bed with a glass of water and drifted away. The next morning, I had to close again and was determined to hit the trail. I was going to run my usual four to six miles before work. I had done this a thousand times before. Laced up my kicks, squeezed into my jogging clothes that had been in a drawer for months, and hit the trail. Oh my god, I was quickly on the verge of throwing up my first mile. What was happening? I used to be the dude whizzing by all the joggers!

Well, I did manage to walk, run, walk, nearly crawl, run, and walk the four miles of my yesteryear. I was proud that I didn't wimp out or listen to my mind say, "Stop!" From there, I made a life commitment to run six days per week (pending injury). And that was just what I did for the next several months. I cut out the diet and energy drinks and got into coffee. I gave all the fast-food joints the bird as I drove by. For me, it was a sensible meal, and the one behavior I did manage to change was that I would always eat lunch. I made time each day to unplug and grab an hour or so for me.

In a rather short period of time, I was actually feeling better. My pants one day were loose on me. (Gents, you know how that feels when your pants dig into your waist all day and you are too shallow and vain to buy larger pants, right? I was the president of this club.) No, really, my pants were loose, and this made me feel great. At my heaviest, I was 238 pounds. I dropped in about a year to 168. Perhaps a bit too thin, but coming from where I was, I was happy.

The key here was I had to make this decision. I had to feel the pain to change. I am not an exercise nut, but I do love to run. My friends think I am a weirdo for running so much, but I really don't care. It saved me. No, correction, I saved me. When I look at the pictures that my wife loves to show nearly everyone, people don't recognize me during the larger years. Besides physical weight, I was mentally overweight too. I wasn't taking care of myself properly, and my mind, body, and soul had no problems telling me so.

I left the company that was the pressure cooker and was recruited to a new company that I guess if you troll my LinkedIn, you can put the pieces together. I interviewed with a gentleman that had a good number of years' experience on me. He was perhaps one the best people I have ever worked with. One of the best things this gent taught me was the fact that there are five days a week to work. We don't have to get everything done today, but most certainly by the end of the week. Totally words to live and work by. (The workaholics will violently disagree. That's fine. They for some reason never seem to finish anything.)

During this time, I was in my early thirties and was learning the art of leading versus doing. A key mentor along the trail, Steve, was just a class act. He, immediately upon hiring me, treated me like a senior guy, very little oversight and tons of empowerment. Our day would start around 8:00 or 8:30 a.m. and finish by 4:30 and with a commute at 6:00 p.m. I had never worked so little in my life and felt so productive. Steve is a guy that lived through the Summer of Love and always chastised me for loving the Grateful Dead. That's okay. He loved Billy Idol, and that should explain everything. (Mr. Idol, I like your songs, just don't love them.) Steve would sometimes pick me up to travel together with the radio on 11 blaring out Billy Idol at 8:00 a.m. Oh, the memories I have.

During our trips in Chicago, North and South Dakota, Steve and I would always take time for lunch and to have some fun. We pheasant hunted together, shot skeet, visited Deadwood and even Mount Rushmore. All while working, delivering great results, building a great team. I was in a leadership and personal developmental chrysalis each day. We traveled nearly every day together for about nine months. Then the company eliminated my position. Steve and his boss wanted to meet with me in person. (Typically, this goes either great or terrible.) Wouldn't you know, I was promoted with a raise in pay. I was no longer working for Steve and now was his peer. I never felt worthy of being his peer then. Today, I still have the deepest respect and fondest memories of learning to have fun at work. Steve grew me up and taught me how to ride the leadership bicycle. I owe a great deal to him. Wait, I took him to the airport one early morning. I think we are even then.

What I want to stress here is that we all have a choice to put forth the right energy and effort to be spiritual and healthy. From whatever you deem right for you, I say do it. Telling yourself and others what you plan on doing versus actually are doing is a major difference. Kind of like this: if you keep one foot in the past and one foot in the future, you are peeing on the present. Visual, I know, but true.

Today, I am the weirdo running in the pouring rain, ninety-five degrees, and blizzard. This one day may do me in, but I am happy doing it. People I work with know that I am a Deadhead, and they also know that I care. I do my very best to remain grounded and humble and try never to spike the football. The title alone to this chapter is a teachable moment. Find your energy out there. Harness your passion and work at it. In life, there are no races. You need to work on enjoying the ride.

CHAPTER FIFTEEN

How to Properly Fail

I didn't fail the test, I just found 100 ways to do it wrong.
—Benjamin Franklin

Oh boy, you achievers out there are going to hate this chapter. For in your mind, failure is certain doom. I don't believe anyone wants to fail. Especially me. However, there is an art to doing so. I hope by now as you continue to read this book, you are realizing the amount of screwups I have collected. Hey, it's okay. Providing we do not fail on purpose, effort counts. So in this chapter, we will take a journey on different types of failure and how to land on your feet (ish).

I think that with every hero in our lives, they at one point experienced failure. It just happens. The real learning comes from failure. Winning feels amazing. Yet it is fleeting too. For once you win, you will most certainly feel the need or even compulsion to win again. I know that I have failed in life and laughed it off and, too, never ever want to feel it again.

Keeping this within the guidelines of retail leadership, I too often see inexperience managers win easy, and this can set them up for quite a fall in the long run. From a responsibility stance, when you are new within management, you were typically promoted for two reasons:

1. You worked hard and were very good at what you were doing. You had gumption, and by golly, why not.
2. You received an education that garnered respect and gave you the opportunity to lead others.

Both of these managers in the examples above don't have any real leading experience. They may have theory but not experience. This is not a bad thing! I am sure they have a belly full of fire and courage. Blending experience with energy is the key to leading a team. However, there will need to be some stumbles along the way. At times, we as evolving leaders do not give ourselves room to fail and set overly ambitions expectations on ourselves and simply will not accept anything but perfect. Sound familiar? (Quit lying, it does.)

Let's start out with the salt-of-the-earth, ground-up manager. (Got a long way to go to grow to a leader.) This is a solid person that has displayed loyalty, competence, results, and an eagerness to grow. There is typically a lot on the line for this person. Family, bills, kids, you know, life. They have a deep sense to provide. They have also worked the ends of the day, endured and gotten used to the clopen, and just have a good head on their shoulders. During their time as an associate or supervisor, they didn't make many mistakes and was the one everyone could count on and go to. In recent times, formal training just sounds better than it is. As long as you know return policies, can count the safe, and arrive to work timely, that could be it.

So what got this hard worker promoted may not be what gets this new manager to find success right? Why not? Hard-worker, team-player, go-to person. As a new manager, this new position requires much different skills than an individual contributor. Without a solid mentor, this new manager is headed for some rocks. It is safe to assume that this new manager will immediately try to replicate what they are personally good at with the new team, right? An example, if this new manager was great at warranty sales or, perhaps, visual presentation, well, why not get a bunch of people that now work for me to do the same?

It is very important to understand that a team is made up of individuals that should have a similar vision and work in a similar manner toward reaching an intended result. Yet the team is not made up of robots, so there will be a bit of zig and zag. By importing what the manager was good at seems logical. However, it may not align with company goals. (If you are feeling like you have one of these people on your team, please breath and go read the 1:1 chapter again.)

If this new manager isn't patient or doesn't see the bigger picture, the new manager may lead the team astray. Get frustrated and lose managerial credibility. For anyone in a new job or position wants to do well. If not closely directed, they will find what they are good at. Or they will not have the competencies to execute the direction and engage the team. You may hear some autocratic language such as "Do your job" or "Because I said so." Super-duper red alarms should ring if you even get a sniff.

The underlying driver here is the fear of failing. Being a manager requires quite a bit of knowledge of the business, and typically most are promoted quickly with little training but "I am here for you" reassurance from their boss.

Let's talk about the recent college graduate. Just devoted four to six years of continuous education with little to no fun at all. (Giggle.) This graduate has studied the history of business theory, finance, accounting, statistics, and even the Roman Empire. Held all kinds of jobs to scrape by in school and now has landed what they believe is the direct line to a corner office with a vice president title by twenty-five. Either drowning in student debt or fortunate to have assistance, they are equally excited to be the boss.

This new manager spends time setting up their office with a framed college degree and a few trinkets from their hobbies and wants to establish themselves as the boss very quickly. For all of professors stressed how important it is to get the team in line for goals and expectations. Now the underlying tone is clearly different here in this example. The fear of failure is much more unknown than the other manager. These two managers have completely different drivers of why they are managers and where they want to go.

Within this example, the college graduate hasn't been promoted but was awarded a well-deserved position. Could there be a bit of proving grounds for the ground-up manager? Any different expectations on these two examples? Let's explore.

The ground-up manager has a tactical advantage. This manager knows the business, the people, and the systems. Light perhaps on business acumen, but has the knowledge to find the right person to get the answers.

The college graduate has quite a bit of experience in modern-day business administration and has studied numerous companies that failed and was able to determine why. I am not trying in any way to compare or give either an advantage here. Just setting up a possible real-life scenario. Question is, when will they start to fail?

Both of these managers have clear advantages over each other. If you combined them both, you may have the perfect person. Yet there is no perfect person, so let's move on.

Failure can come at any time. Predicted, spontaneous, even from left field. The key here is building a team that can handle failure and won't be hesitant to keep pushing forward in the face of challenge. This is why a leader must allow a bit of failure. Within the two manager examples, they are new and eager. They will want to do everything perfect, early, and under budget. They haven't professionally failed yet and do not know the warning signs. Warning signs? You mean, we can be aware of possible failure? Sure can. Here are some examples that I have experienced:

1. The ultimate goal to be no. 1 at everything. This is a snare trap that gets many managers and leaders. Remember how great winning feels? Hearing your name as no. 1, a pat on the back, a bonus, or a promotion! How could this be a warning sign? There is only one World Series, Super Bowl, Indy 500, or to these completely insane and brave souls, UFC winner. Does that mean that everyone else in football, baseball, motor sports, or the UFC are losers? Technically, yes. However, in reality, no way! Yes, all these teams work their tails off to win it all. But only one team or fighter shall be crowned the winner. Imagine if we lived our lives this fiercely? First person or nothing to checkout at the gro-

cery store. First person or nothing to pick up the kids at school. Life would be insanely quick. Being no. 1 is great. However, inspiring a team to behave and perform toward a no. 1 goal is great too. (I am sure the losers of the World Series are paid quite well.) And to that point, the winners are no better people than the losers. They just scored more points during a game. That's all. Both teams have families, friends, and dreams of probably being no. 1.

2.   Win at all costs. Many of the companies I have worked for offer a year-end incentive of Circle of Champions getaway for the best of the best. Now oftentimes, these are the very best leaders that devoted themselves to their jobs, their teams, and their results. They earned a fabulous trip to the Caribbean or Mexico with the senior leaders. They even earned all the free swag they get (new set of clubs, watches, trinkets of sort). I have always given a standing O to these leaders of amazement. Seriously, I have. On the other side of this sharp coin is the manager who swindled their way to no. 1, broke rules, or just plain lucked out on an easy sales plan. This is deadly, for they return from this trip of champions with the actual thought that they earned this title. They wear their champion title like a Roman helmet. They become more of what got them to this position. A total arrogant, selfish asshole. They have no idea in reality how they fell into no. 1, but boy, did the fruit of victory taste great. So their goal for next year is to repeat. Thing is, they don't know how, so they press the living crap out of their team for themselves and not the good of the business nor morale of the team. If ever the rubber stamp of failure is coming closer and closer, I do not know of any better example. Strangely, I rarely saw any of these champions get promoted or move to higher roles. They mainly stayed journeymen store leaders and bounced around from company to company. In their wake was littered with the bodies of former leaders they fired to get to no. 1. Most of

these types of managers feel that thinning the herd is the only way to get to no. 1.

Lesson? Hell yes there is one here. Winning is again what we should all strive to do every day. How to win is just as important as failing. One must handle each of these very carefully. There are lessons to learn in both. Choosing not to will lead to more blind failure. My personal rule for success is that if my team is growing, I am growing. If my team is winning, I am winning, and if my team delivers top-notch results, well, great for them. We earned it. Whatever trinket I may earn holds nothing to the feeling of watching leaders mature and perform. Big picture, you are going to fail quite a bit in your life. Deal with it and learn from it. The very best of the best in this world are pretty darn good at it. Do you remember the 1986 Super Bowl Champs? I don't and frankly don't care. Because once the team won and confetti settled, the broadcasters were already prognosticating who was going to be champs next year. The circle of winning never ends, and it is like the damnation of Tantalus and his eternal quest for water to quench his thirst. It never ends. Enjoy the little wins and learn from the losses, and in the end, we all may be just fine.

CHAPTER SIXTEEN

You Must Set Your Personal Constitution

As a leader, you will have a code of ethics policy and a general handbook of policies and procedures within your company. These are very basic and act as guardrails to ensure most employees abide by common sense. Follow these to the tee, and if ever I could give you advice, always take a partner for large issues. Your HR leader will thank you very much for doing so. A majority of these policies will give you the tools to be successful when dealing with "stuff." Yet there is more to it than a P&P handbook. There needs to be some gut instincts that navigate the foggy waters. The title alone gives strength to what I want to teach. A constitution is pretty darn important and should be solid as a rock.

Too many times when I took over a team, a store, a district, or even a region, I would quickly identify the haves and the have-nots. Typically, metrics are a good place to start. I could easily see through trend analysis who is making a difference and, well, who needs some encouragement. When I would visit with the teams, I would connect the dots from metrics to behaviors. In all, no boss ever taught me this technique. It just sort of happened one day. After metrics, behaviors, store standards, and well-crafted responses, I would rely on my constitution. Here are some bullet points of mine:

- Be nice to people.
- Say please and thank you.

- Make eye contact.
- Talk more about your team's positive attributes than yours.
- Open the door for people.
- Iron your clothes and shine your shoes.
- Know your business. (Don't feel the need to memorize, but know your biz.)
- Help everyone, not just the bosses.
- Spend time with new hires.
- Get to know what drives your team members.
- Be nice to animals.
- Talk to everyone as if your mama was standing next to you.
- Recognize the heck out of wins.
- Always coach in private and be honest.
- Get shopping carts from the parking lot.
- Don't forget how you felt when you were new.
- Listen more than you speak.
- Stay humble.

Think you get the point, right? These mean quite a bit to me. I am not perfect in all these, and my mother would probably give me a good whack every now and then when I slip up and swear. (Don't worry, I deserve it.) Big picture, I observe my team on how they fall within these guidelines. At no time do I impart this on to them, but I simply just observe. If one of my leaders falls out of line with one or more of these, I will share my thoughts with them. Here is an example: "Say, Danielle, I noticed that in our last staff meeting you were a bit course with the new manager, Phil. May I ask what drove you to speak over him?" I am direct in my feedback and offer a gentle question to allow the leader to respond. I want her to realize that I am observing her behavior and that I care enough to share my observations. My goal isn't to demoralize the leader but offer constructive feedback. More importantly, be vague enough to get her thinking on an alternative approach. I am generally not a hammer to the face kind of leader. I tend to inspire thought versus reaction.

No matter the situation, if you learn to develop a constitution, and I repeat, *and* follow the company's policies and procedures, you should be A-OK. If ever in doubt, get a partner. Oftentimes I receive calls from leaders asking how they should deal with an employee or situation. It becomes very clear if the presenting leader has developed their constitution. Here are some examples:

"Hi, Brian, I wanted to share with you that Tom in housewares is dating one of my managers. I know the policy states that managers are not permitted to date associates, but in this case, they never work together and rarely see each other. Is this okay?"

"Brian, one of my associates just told a customer to go to hell. You know, the customer was being very rude and wanted to return a product from six months ago!"

"Hey, Brian, I want to write up my assistant manager for always being late."

As clear as these examples are, they can all be solved within the company's policies and procedures. However, in none of the examples was the manager secure in their decision nor utilized their own critical thinking to make a decision. More, they were impulsive and perhaps emotional. As you mature and get more life experience, you tend to build a stronger constitution. You can rely on great decisions you have made and also avoid the doozies too. Let's rethink these three scenarios with a stronger and employed constitution:

"Hi, Brian, I just learned that one of my managers is dating an associate in the housewares department. This is clearly a violation of our fraternization policy, and I have confirmed it through a meeting with my assistant and the manager in question. My manager admitted and just started this relationship. I feel it is the store and company's best interest to transfer this manager to another location immediately. I have spoken to a peer, and he is in need of the very position. I wanted to partner with you to let you know my course of action. How do you feel about my plan?"

Good!

"Brian, sorry to bother you, but I am calling to let you know that I have already partnered with our HR team and just terminated an associate that used foul language directly to their face. This is just 100 percent unacceptable and obviously against our policy on customer service. There is no action needed from you, but as a professional courtesy, I wanted you to be in the loop. I will use this as a teachable moment with my team."

Impressive!

"Hello, Brian, I have a manager that I am coaching routinely for being tardy to work. I sat him down and spoke with him regarding this problem. Boy, am I glad I did. Bill shared with me that his car is broken down and he doesn't have the money to get it fixed. He is walking to work every day, and it is over four miles. He was embarrassed to say that when he gets to work, he is drenched with sweat and goes to the neighbor store next to us to clean up. This is why he is late. I called our associate assistance fund, and they are helping him with the car repair bills. Wow, I am super proud to be a part of this team."

Real life.

It is always easier to take the direct route to a destination. However, at times, the destination is the actual journey of learning. Rather zen, I know, but imagine the impact we as leaders have on our teams, their families, and even their pets. Just because we have the sword of justice does not mean we need to use it.

In review, this chapter is a bit preachy, I know. The bullet points above may have been a bit too much. Yet the spirit of this book is to inspire you to be you! To do that, you must get to know you better. You certainly don't have to agree with me on everything, but the intent is to share and get you thinking. You'll find the right answers.

CHAPTER SEVENTEEN

How to Properly Take a Vacation

This chapter is dedicated to all the brave men and women who feel the need to work while on vacation. You are so important that your team cannot exist for three weeks out of the year without you. The world is better because of you.

Hope I wasn't too sarcastic. In reality, I used to be one of these brave, eh, not-so-organized, and potentially a bit egotistical managers. Yes. I brought my laptop to Florida too many times to count.

"Dad, do you want to go swimming?"

"Ah, yeah, in just a moment. I am sending an e-mail, Aiden."

Really? An e-mail? Little did I know that for the hour or so I took to selfishly check unimportant email, Aiden stood patiently and waited. I looked up and saw him standing there just staring at me. I felt terrible. I knew I was wrong and too was being self-absorbed. It took a six-year-old to teach me that lesson.

Let's examine why companies offer benefits such as vacation time. Hmmmm, to give employees paid time off to use as they wish. Meaning time away from work. Not time away from work working. So why do so many of us bring the office with us on vacation? Simple. To stay connected and feel important. No matter your response, this is the reason. Deeper analysis is needed.

There are primarily two reasons we don't take restful, unplugged vacations. 1. Ego—We feel we are so important that we feel we need to work while vacation. As mentioned before, this sends a message of insecurity to your team. Trust me, you aren't that important. Even though currently, you may feel so. 2. Total lack of organization. If you cannot stay on top of work and let it bleed over to vacation, well then what message does this send? Let's dig a bit deeper:

Staying Connected

With technology these days, it is pretty much impossible to fully disconnect. Unless you turn your phone off and hide the charger. Our phones are our lifelines. They control it all. When you hear the ping of an e-mail, the temptation is so great to read it. You almost treat it like you are doing something wrong when you do. Many of us work on teams and within teams require teamwork and team communication. So how in the world can I not answer the e-mail? Simple again, don't. If you do, you are setting the precedence that working on vacation is acceptable. Even the smallest response possible gives this notion a green light. Set your out of office and a good contact to call if there is an emergency and enjoy your vacation. The work will be there when you return, promise.

Feeling Important

I will start with myself here. When I became a field leader and was given a smartphone and a laptop, I felt I was nearly a CEO. I mean, look at this swag! Gadgets! Little did I know that these sons of B—— would never stop making noises! I would often decry. I got at least a hundred e-mails a day! Like anyone cared, I had to make sure you knew it. Planes, trains, and yes, cars, I would have my laptop open and banging away on e-mails. I soon looked in the mirror and found the majority of my time was being spent on e-mail and not with the great people in the stores! We all want to feel important, and that is a good thing. We want to be counted on. We want to serve our teams. However, we are not that important to give up time with family, friends, and loved ones to work on a computer while on vacation.

One of the questions I often ask people I work with is, "Where are you planning a vacation?" It interests me to learn where people go. From staycations to cruises, I like to see people light up when they share their dreams and plans. As a leader, keep this in mind: listen more than you talk. You can learn quite a bit about your team members if you ask questions about how they like to have fun. In the end, you will not remember the vast amount of calls and meetings you attended. However, you will never forget that time on the beach when you mooned that boat full of tourists like you.

Here is another hard and fast rule. If you are a leader that earns four weeks of vacation, take it. That is one week per quarter. I cannot tell you how many people I have met that say gracefully "Man, I can never take all of my vacation time" or "I usually lose a week of vacation each year." Why? Vacations are not cheap, but staying home for a week to recharge is always a good idea. This goes again to the thought of being unorganized or the need to always feel important. Remember, you are important, and you cast a large shadow as a leader. Success is not defined by being connected 100 percent of the time. Growing a team to work collectively to take the reins when needed makes everything work.

So start planning your next getaway and enjoy yourself. You are becoming a leader. You will need your rest.

CHAPTER EIGHTEEN

Fear

When a resolute young fellow steps up to the great bully,
the world, and takes him boldly by the beard, he is often
surprised to find it comes off in his hand, and that it was
only tied on to scare away the timid adventurers.
—Ralph Waldo Emerson

As we get closer to the end of this book, I want to spend some time on a topic that affects us all. No matter what, we all have some type of fear. When handled correctly, fear can actually keep us sharp. Yet too many times we let fear wiggle into our mind, and boy, can it warp the truth. Take a moment before you continue to read and think of what you might be fearful of right now. Then try to think of what specifically you are afraid of. (Keep this in mind as you read on.)

I have lived with some sort of fear my whole life. I know I'm not unique in this statement, for we all have. Question is, why? Fear isn't a physical element, more it tends to be a belief of what may or may not happen. I want to direct this chapter on how fear is often used for and against leaders.

Have you ever had a boss that used intimidation as the motivator? "If you ever think you are going to get promoted, you better do a better job." "I work well past my shifts to get more done. Why don't you?" These two statements are most likely said daily in some sort of way. And they both totally suck. What kind of manager says this? For they are impersonal, are nonspecific, and make you wonder. That is exactly the moment fear enters your mind. When we wonder about anything, we tend to go right to the fear side. You know, right after an interview or a date. "Did I impress them?" Even asking this internal question is fraught with error. You can never get an honest answer until you actually get one. Until then, we tend to think of every possible method of our demise. Let's look at some typical areas of fear in retail:

- My best leader may quit at any time.
- We are never going to make our sales budget.
- I think my boss doesn't like me.
- Why haven't they answered my e-mail? Are they mad at me?
- Will I ever get a promotion?
- I know layoffs are coming.

Ugh, all time wasters! Imagine if you worked and led every day without any fear. What could you accomplish? (For me, I can't get past spiders, so I cannot say *any*.) Being that you can only control the present and not the future, why not dedicate yourself 100 percent to making the present fun and rewarding. Too often, nearly everything we do is due to some sort of fear.

For me, I was chin deep in fear for a large portion of my early leadership roles. I mean, I was always working around people that were afraid, so in turn, I became afraid. I really didn't know what I was afraid of, but darn it, I was afraid of being not afraid! Seriously, when I reflect on the vast amounts of people I have met, I can maybe name two or three that really, and I mean really, walked in their own shoes. They came to work and made it happen. These intrepid souls were not mavericks but secure. They didn't wear the latest trends or focus on superficial crap. They were their own people. We will get to learning behaviors such as these in just a bit.

I also have worked for leaders that have absolutely no problem leading with fear and fear alone. I will share a story.

I was a robust twenty-three-year-old department leader and was feeling pretty good at being pretty good. okay, I was cocky as hell.

However, in full disclosure, I have and will always appreciated and respected the associates who bust their tails each and every day. I was more cocky to other managers. Trust me, I was. I wore clothes I couldn't afford and drove a car that was ridiculously too expensive. However, I wanted an image. I paid more attention to my appearance than my actual work. I was making $30,000, and I looked like lawyer. Way over my skis! I did this for one reason: fear of not fitting in. However, by doing this, I completely did not fit in! No one around me dressed like me, and too, no one around me did not behave like me. I guess if I just had been me, I would have been just fine.

Right around this time, there was a new store manager named Bill. Bill was from a big city, and he was a no-nonsense dude. The kind of guy who really didn't care about formalities like "Hello." Bill came to our store, and he started to change everything! I mean everything. In no time, everyone simply hated him. Me being me, I warmed up to Bill and was able to have a two-sentence conversation with him. Within a month, he had a nice nickname for me: Loser.

Bill was direct, and for once, I really appreciated it. I never had to wonder about anything. Yeah, he was as subtle as a raging bull, but easy to work with. Do your job and do it well, and you're fine. Then one day, he came up to me with pumpkin eyes and said the regional manager was on his way. Being a noob manager, I didn't get the panic. Bill was actually speaking to me and asking me how the store looked and if I was ready.

"Ready for what, sir?"

"For the regional manager!"

Ignorantly, I responded with, well, "Hell yes!"

Bill somewhat had a sense of comfort in my pithy response.

The regional manager, Rick, showed up in his company car and pressed suit. (Yes, in those days, we wore suits to work. Can you even tie a tie? Questionable at best.) I was positioned at the front door as the greeter and first responder. Wait, I didn't even know what the regional manager, or RM, looked like. Well, anyone walking up to the store in a suit is the RM for sure.

I think Bill was in the back of the store either throwing up or thinking of clever responses to any question he might gather. I greeted Rick and, being a young fella, said, "Welcome, sir! We have been waiting for you."

Rick responded with, "How did you know I was coming?"

"Bill told me."

Rick scoffed at me and started to walk toward the offices. Big picture, I had no idea why Rick was at our store. I was just enamored for him being here. Bill and Rick walked the store, and I literally saw sweat coming from Bill. Nothing looked troublesome, but it did look intense.

After about an hour, Rick walked up to me and said, "Young man, I hear good things about you. Keep up the good work."

"Thank you, Rick."

Then he was gone. Dude, why all the fuss? Bill had a list of things to fix, and he looked at me and said, "I hope you don't have plans tonight."

"No, just going jogging when I get home."

"Good. We are in for a long night."

Getting back to current times, whoa. I will always have a some-what warm place in my heart for Bill, but he was wound tight. I left that store shortly after and moved to Chicago. Never heard or saw Bill again.

When you think of fear, this story gives us retail folks that have lived this crisis credibility. Why do we freak out when visitors come? For me, I have always, and I do promise always, felt honored to get a visit. I have done my best to learn from these folks and get to know them. In turn, I have fostered good and lasting relationship with many leaders senior to I. Not that I am better or clever, just personable at best. I have had my rear handed to me in a visit and completely failed. But I have made the most of challenging times.

You know, I have been accused of being cocky through my life, and honestly, I am going to be bold, but I am not. I do not want to beat anyone, and I really don't care about rankings. I am genuinely myself, and I feel this has made others at all levels, mind you, inse-cure. "Why isn't this guy nervous?" Because I choose not to be. That is it. If you right now are in fear of something, no matter work, life, health, or wealth, kick it in the ass with confidence. No one can beat you but you. Yeah, in sports, you can get whooped. Maybe, well definitely in a fight, but in your mind, you own this. Do your best to work away from what others deem is frightful. We are all in this together, and when you start letting fear in, you immediately lose. It is perfectly fine to be nervous. This keeps us honest and on point. But if anyone was to tell me that I scare them, this would be a total mistake on me.

You are unique and bring a unique set of talents to everything you do. Trust yourself, push yourself, and whatever you do, do not grade yourself compared to others. This limits growth. It is cool that others around you may do so. Play the game, but in your heart and mind, own it. Do not give anything to anyone in terms of your fear. If you hear a statement from a manager such as "You'd better improve or else I will have to make a tough decision," just rest assured this statement was made in ignorance. For a leader would step in and help. A manager will stay at a safe distance and make threats. A leader goes shoulder to shoulder and helps you each step of the way. You are an evolving leader. Be sure to keep this in mind.

Okay, closure to fear. It is not an off-and-on kind of thing. New stuff, crazy stuff, immediate stuff, and sudden stuff will all have fear attached. It is our choice what to do with fear when we get it. None of us are superhuman, but all of us have the ability to choose. Dismiss it. Meh. Yawn. Kick its ass. That's the lesson here. Damn, I am proud of you already.

The next time you come in contact with fear, I will be watching how you handle it!

CHAPTER NINETEEN

You're Bleepin' Awesome

Well, they tell me of a pie up in the sky, waiting for me when I die.
—Jimmy Cliff

Being awesome requires great responsibility. It requires you to be you. I for one am proud of you! While we haven't met just yet, you have taken time to learn from someone else. You now have learned the difference between a manager and a leader, and I promise you that you will start to size up people you meet going forward. You now have a nose for leadership.

You are going to fail. You will totally screw things up. This is life. Permitting you never fail on purpose, this is called growth. The best part of you is you, so be authentic and always have the mind-set "I am growing." You know, I meet many great people who just cannot take a win for what it is—a win. They always feel the need to be better or not to appreciate where they are. Darn sad if you ask me. Good example is that a great leader I know recently ran a half marathon. They ran in under two hours and paced an eight-minute mile. For roughly 99 percent of the population, this is near superhuman. For this leader, the remark after the race was "I can do better." Really? I am sure you can shave off a few minutes, but have you looked at the big picture? You just ran a half marathon! Now this person is a fantastic individual and a leader of leaders. I appreciate the winning mind-set. However, personally, if they do not give themselves the feeling of a win, then have they won? I personally love this statement for now I have more fodder to poke fun at. "Hmm, 143rd place out of 500? Guess only 142 runners are better than you." You get the picture.

I mean, you are bleepin' awesome! You will need to keep this phrase front and center at times for you will feel defeated and even bested. This is okay. Oftentimes, this just conjures more energy to train or study harder the next time. If we won everything we attempted, we would quickly lose steam to try. Believing in yourself and then having a positive mental picture of yourself does not mean you are arrogant! It means you believe in yourself and are proud of yourself! Big difference.

So how in the heck are you going to apply some of these rather amazing learnings you have read in this book? (Pardon the self-adulation in the previous sentence.) I suggest you do absolutely nothing for a few days. Yup, nada. Let your brain start to connect some dots and give this some thought. No, this isn't the annual convention at your company that you need to leave and do everything differently and perfectly to start the new year. No, this is foundational belief and development. You might not have read a book in a while or, perhaps, not the strongest in constant learning. This too is okay. The fact that we are here together is the win. After a few days, you will have some good ideas as to the hows and whys. How do you want to go about some large evolution to your approach, and why is it necessary? What will it make an impact on, and who will be better for it?

I have attended many different meetings and conferences. I too have listened to people with far greater success than I. Perhaps one of the most compelling speakers I had the pleasure to listen to was Jim Kelly, the former NFL Buffalo Bills quarterback. Jim spoke of his vast success as a professional football player and the rigors of competing at that level. Then he became the most down-to-earth, humble, and heartfelt person when he spoke of his son, Hunter, and how he battled an illness that eventually took his life. Jim spoke to us all about the difference between work and family and how we as leaders must not only look at our teams this way but ourselves this way. I was in awe. How could such a heroic athlete be so humble and giving? Jim's story was inspirational for me, and I know everyone else, because he was able to say his family was more important than football. Life lesson.

This book will most likely not change your life. My intent was to make you laugh, inspire you to be open-minded, and get you thinking about yourself and where you are at right now. Is there room to grow? Do I need to fundamentally change? Can I? Should I? Will I? All these rest on your shoulders. An annual performance review typically will not do this. You need some quiet time to think about your current situation and how you can grow from here on out. If you have lots of work to do, think of this book as a cast on a broken arm. The cast simply keeps the arm in place, and the real healing comes from the inside. If you were forced to read this book, well, good. You probably have an amazing leader that cares about you.

Retail leaders today do not have a smooth road. The amount of competition, omnichannel, and just a foundational shift in consumer buying is making nearly everyone freak out. This obviously rolls to the brave teams in the stores. We in the stores, however, are the heartbeat of the company. Remember, we are leading the charge face-to-face with the customer. You as the former manager and now evolving leader must nurture and grow the skills of your team to outexecute the store team across the street. If you take this book to heart and apply the learnings, I cannot guarantee success, but I will say that you will make a difference and be a leader that your team will never forget. The impression that you will make will last in the minds of your team. You too will grow and most likely become a leader of leaders. No matter your title, we all have one common goal: success. This is both personal and professional.

Now it is up to you. Go make it happen. Be different. Be you!

EPILOGUE

Writing this book was a journey for me. It was written over the course of five years and many different periods within my life. I am a thankful person and probably say this too much, but thank you for taking the time to read this book. When I was deep into writing, I would often share my energy with my friends and family about writing this book. I would usually get an odd retort, "Really? Let me know when it is done. I want to read it." I will validate this statement with the metrics of sales and conversations! My passion is to teach and inspire. My job is to police and get compliance. These two rarely meet. My vision from here is to form a leadership coaching company. I want to take leaders and those pesky managers to my academy for a few days of fun in the sun. Scratch that, intense leadership schooling. From lecture to team discussion to experiential rigorous education. I'm talking 2:00 a.m. night hikes with each student having the opportunity to lead us in the dead of night. While very few leaders will ever do this at the store or office, they will be able to reflect and rely on their experience versus theory. I too have dreams. I also want to thank all the friends and family members who received a call from me at all times of the day and night to give me feedback on my writing. From the laughs to at times a tear or two, it all matters.

I plan on writing more in the future. The first book is filled with blind corners and dark spots. This is the fun stuff! In addition, this book serves as an example of how a dream can be turned into reality. I always loved to write as a kid and then got busy as an adult. However, if you have a dream of doing something, all you have to do is start it one day. Then give it some more work the next, and before you know it, you are done and accomplished. I am sure that not everyone will believe in my thoughts and learnings. Good for you. You are entitled to your own thoughts. For the ones that you took too, keep at it. Your team craves a consistent leader and one who makes work fun. Your boss will definitely see a new edge to you. Do not let anyone talk you away from leading and inspiring!

ABOUT THE AUTHOR

Brian Travilla is a retail leader with over twenty-five years' experience, from his start as a paint mixer for a department store to now leading thousands of leaders and associates for a number of companies. Brian takes a ground-up approach to earning your stripes with your team and why a good pair of shoes makes the difference. Throughout his career, spanning varying retailers with multiple specialties, Brian has always stayed true to his core belief on why leadership is the single factor that makes the difference. Brian and his wife, Charlene, and sons, Nicolas, Aiden, and Parker, along with their golden retriever, Pippen, live in the suburbs of Chicago.

CPSIA information can be obtained
at www.ICGtesting.com
Printed in the USA
LVHW050005240919
631983LV00003B/626/P

9 781643 507682